ST GEORGE

ST GEORGE

Let's Hear it for England!

ALISON MALONEY

preface
publishing

Published by Preface Publishing 2010

10 9 8 7 6 5 4 3 2 1

Copyright © Alison Maloney 2010

Alison Maloney has asserted her right to be identified as the author of this
work under the Copyright, Designs and Patents Act 1988

First published in Great Britain in 2010 by Preface Publishing
20 Vauxhall Bridge Road
London SW1V 2SA

An imprint of The Random House Group Limited

www.rbooks.co.uk
www.prefacepublishing.co.uk

Addresses for companies within The Random House Group Limited
can be found at www.randomhouse.co.uk

The Random House Group Limited Reg. No. 954009

A CIP catalogue record for this book is available from the British Library

ISBN 978 1 84809 262 4

Mixed Sources
Product group from well-managed
forests and other controlled sources
www.fsc.org Cert no. TT-COC-2139
© 1996 Forest Stewardship Council

The Random House Group Limited supports The Forest Stewardship Council
(FSC), the leading international forest certification organisation. All ourtitles that
are printed on Greenpeace approved FSC certified paper carry the FSC logo. Our
paper procurement policy can be found at www.rbooks.co.uk/environment

Printed and bound in Great Britain by Clays Ltd, St Ives PLC

For Dad with love

Our language is England's greatest gift to the world . . . and this is the week to celebrate it

by

Boris Johnson

First published 19 April 2009 in the *Daily Mail*

NOT LONG AGO City Hall in London put out a modest press announcement about our plans for St George's Day – and we couldn't believe the reaction.

The phones went wild. The emails and the letters started to swamp our response teams.

People started crossing the road to shake my hand, pumping it up and down and thanking me with embarrassing fervour.

I felt like some Texan prospector who has idly whacked his pickaxe on some piece of unpromising ground and then stood back in amazement before a great gusher of erupting oil.

As I studied some of the emails I got a sense of pent-up longing, of people who were yearning to reclaim the English flag from the extremists.

They didn't want anything to do with the far right. They deeply disliked the BNP.

They didn't want to cock a snook at the Scots, and they didn't have any particular resentment of the Welsh or the Irish.

They certainly didn't have any hostility towards St Patrick's Day, or Diwali or any of the other high days and holy days we mark in the great multi-ethnic metropolis.

They just felt that London was not only the capital of Britain, and of the United Kingdom, but also the capital of England.

After decades of watching ceremonies and festivals in honour of just about everyone, they wanted to celebrate the genius of England on the day of England's patron saint.

In a simple, joyful and unthreatening way – in a way that included all the communities that live here – they wanted a day to announce their pride in this country and all the things it has given the world.

Now at this point we must be careful, because when politicians try to analyse the particular genius of England, they notoriously come unstuck.

In 1924, Stanley Baldwin made a lyrical speech extolling the things he believed were the imperishable and eternal about England.

He spoke of the cry of the corncrake, and the tinkle of the anvil in the country smithy, and the sight of a plough-

man and his team of horses coming over the brow of a hill —
a sight, he said, that would exist as long as England was a
land.

Well, I bet there is not a single reader who has heard the
tinkle of an anvil in a smithy recently, still less seen a ploughman with his horses — and you'd have to get up pretty early
these days to hear a corncrake.

John Major fared little better when he announced that the
essence of England consisted in warm beer, the shades
lengthening on county cricket pitches, and old maids cycling
through the morning mist to communion.

Everybody speedily pointed out that people were switching
from warm beer to lager, that many county cricket grounds now
had floodlights, and what with churches being deconsecrated
all over the country, the sight of an old maid cycling to
communion — with or without the morning mist — was
becoming about as common as the cry of the corncrake.

Asked to define the genius of the country, both Tony Blair
and Gordon Brown have desperately mumbled something
about the NHS.

To which people have said: 'Yes, the health service is a
wonderful institution, but wasn't England a magical country
before 1948?'

So what is it, my friends, that makes up the special genius of
England? What is it that people will be coming out to celebrate
on St George's Day?

Some people say it is all about democracy, and a sense of fair play, and a love of gardening – and all that is true.

But they have some decent gardens in Holland, the Danes have always seemed to me to have a keen sense of fair play and the Icelandic parliament is probably older than our own.

Some say it is about pubs, and an obsession with the weather, and yes, it is true that there is something very English about the beery breath of a pub on a hot bank holiday and we certainly like to bang on about the weather.

But can these really be said to amount to the quintessence of Englishness, when so many pubs are closing down, and when our weather patterns – far from being unique – are actually the same as those of Ireland, Holland, New Zealand and most of northern France?

Some say it is all about embarrassment and irony and our special gift of humour, and again, there is something in that.

Many foreign beaches will be treated this summer to the immortal sight of the Englishman trying to change into his swimming trunks with the help of a towel, and falling over.

But then you look at Jonathan Ross and Russell Brand, and you wonder whether we are quite as full of embarrassment and gentle irony as we once were.

So what is it, then? What is the supreme gift of the English to the rest of the world? The answer, dear reader, is under your nose.

The genius of England resides to some extent in all the things we have so far discussed.

But if there is one thing that marks us out and defines us, it is the language, the greatest, the most fertile and the most stunningly successful language the world has ever seen.

The Germans may beat us at music; the Italians have the edge in painting – but the English beat all comers at poetry, and that is why it is right that we should celebrate St George's Day in April.

It is not only the month that inspired Chaucer and T S Eliot. On 23 April we also mark the birth of William Shakespeare, the man who mobilised that language more effectively than anyone before or since.

So why is English so formidable? Why does it knock Mandarin into a cocked hat? Because it has twice as many words as either French or German.

There are 500,000 words in the dictionary, and that is because it is a confluence of the two great streams of Romance and Anglo-Saxon.

It is a mongrel language, a language that shamelessly and brilliantly continues to absorb imports from around the world. That is why it is so fitting that St George is himself an import. Like my ancestors, it turns out he was a Turk, and it is testament to the generosity of the English that we have made him our saint.

According to Gibbon, he had nothing to do with a dragon, but was a Cappadocian merchant who made a fortune selling bacon to the Roman army.

What could be more appropriate? Napoleon said the English were a nation of shopkeepers.

He meant it as an insult. We take it as a compliment. It is that spirit of small-business entrepreneurship that encouraged St George to flog his bacon to the Romans and will lead this country out of recession.

So come on out and celebrate the multi-faceted genius of this country, and cry God for Harry, England and St George the seller of bacon!

Reproduced by kind permission of Boris Johnson

Contents

St George – Let's Hear it for England!

I N HIS REASSESSMENT of the legends of saints in AD 494, sceptic Pope Gelasius described St George as one of those 'whose names are rightly reverenced among us, but whose actions are known only to God'. The story of England's patron saint is so encased in myth and legend that the truth of his remarkable life is unknown. To most he is a mythical brave knight and a symbol of the triumph of good over evil. To those who know more about his Christian legend, he is a martyr who defended his faith through horrendous tortures at the hands of the Romans. Yet, despite his position as the figurehead of England, more than a quarter of those now living in the country could not name their patron saint and fewer still could name the date of St George's Day.

In many ways the attitude of the English to their patron saint reflects the many contradictions in the story of St George and the growth of his legend worldwide. A Christian martyr from Turkey, murdered by a Roman emperor in Palestine, he is a legendary dragon slayer who saved a virgin princess from sacrifice – but not before insisting her entire town converted to Christianity. Yet he is also the model for mythical Islamic hero al-Khidr and revered by Muslims in the Middle East. He is the patron saint of England but never set foot on English soil and the legend of his chivalrous deeds came from the imagination of an Italian bishop.

While a committed Christian, he is depicted as a warrior and was said to have appeared on the battlefield during the crusades and, as such, he is patron saint of soldiers, cavalry, archers, horses and chivalry and Boy Scouts. Yet his martyrdom and resurrection means he is linked to healing and rebirth, and is celebrated throughout Europe when the first shoots of spring appear, and he is patron saint of field workers and farmers. His healing credentials have also awarded him the patronage of those afflicted by leprosy, plague and syphilis. At the same time, while we claim him as our own, he is revered all over the world and is patron saint of Aragon, Catalonia, Georgia, Lithuania, Ethiopia, Palestine, Portugal, Germany, Greece, Moscow, Istanbul, Genoa and Venice.

The cult of St George took seven centuries to arrive in England from its origins in the Middle East, and the dragon legend didn't emerge until some 200 years after that, in around 1260. His popularity reached a peak in the Middle Ages, beginning to decline again during the Reformation of the Church in Europe in the sixteenth century. The formation of Great Britain and the introduction of the Union Flag meant the saint, and his red cross ensign, sank further into obscurity, and the twentieth century saw his imagery being hijacked by the far right for racist rather than patriotic causes.

In recent years, through national pride more than religious fervour, the popularity of St George's Day has risen sharply, with more parades, parties and pub get-togethers than we saw in the latter half of the twentieth century. Euro '96 saw the cross of St George reclaimed as the mark of the English sports fan and patriot rather than the badge of prejudice, and the devolution of Scotland and Wales meant a resurgence in English patriotism and renewed calls for pride in the national identity.

After a long time on the sidelines, St George is back in fashion. But what is behind the myth? Did St George actually exist or was he merely the hero in an epic tale of derring-do invented by a fertile medieval imagination?

The following pages look at the facts, the legends and the worldwide fame of the patron saint of England.

CHAPTER ONE

George the Dragon Slayer

I have little doubt that when St George had killed the
dragon he was heartily afraid of the princess.

G K CHESTERTON, *The Victorian Age in Literature*

THE STORY OF St George's battle with the dragon has
been told to children throughout Europe since the
thirteenth century. It is the stuff of fairy tales,
featuring a damsel in distress, a heartbroken king and the
chivalrous knight who comes to her rescue and slaughters a
deadly predator.

Where better to begin then, than with the story itself.

Long ago, in the town of Silene, in the country of Libya, in
a deep wide lake, lived a fearsome dragon which had terrorised
the entire country with his venomous breath. The people of the
town had banded together to slay him but had fled in fear on
each attempt. Instead, to pacify him and keep him well fed,
they sacrificed two sheep every night.

When this failed to stop the dragon's attacks on the town, a
meeting was held and it was decided that the children would be

offered to the dragon one by one, and the sacrifice chosen by a lottery system, regardless of wealth and status.

In time, the lot fell on the royal princess and the king was distraught, begging the townspeople to spare her. 'For God's sake,' he told them, 'take gold and silver and all that I have, and let me have my daughter.'

But the townspeople were angry, telling him, 'You made the law, and our children are dead, but you would break the law to save your own. Your daughter shall be given, or else we shall burn you and your house.'

Weeping, he begged for eight days' respite to be with his daughter, and when the eight days were up, the people came to him and said, 'The time has come, the city is perishing.' The king dressed his beautiful daughter in a wedding gown, kissed her and led her to the lake where the dragon lay.

As she awaited her fate, the young knight George passed by and asked her what she was doing there and why she was weeping.

'Be on your way, young man,' she told him, 'so that you do not perish with me.'

But George would not leave her so she told her tearful tale.

'Fair daughter,' George told her, 'fear not. I will help you in the name of Jesus Christ.' Again she begged him to spare himself but the gallant knight would not be daunted.

As they spoke, the terrible beast rose from his slumber and began to lumber towards them. George drew his sword, leapt onto his horse and, after making the sign of the Cross, charged the dragon. A fierce battle ensued and the brave knight smote the dragon with his spear, badly wounding it.

'Take off your girdle and place it around the dragon's neck,' he told the sobbing princess. 'Do not be afraid.'

The cowed creature was led into the town square but the frightened people took one look and fled to the hills, screaming, 'We'll all be dead.'

'Do not fear,' George told them. 'If you believe in God and Jesus Christ, and are baptised into the faith, I will slay the dragon.' The king and all the townsfolk were overjoyed and readily agreed to be baptised, and the virtuous hero duly cut off the dragon's head and ordered that its body be thrown into the surrounding fields.

Fifteen thousand men were baptised, and many more women and children, and the king vowed to build a church in the town to honour St George. Within its walls flowed a fountain with the miraculous power to heal the sick.

The king offered the victorious knight as much money as he liked, but he refused, asking instead that it be given to the poor. He entreated the king to look after the churches, honour the priests, attend regular services and to have pity on the poor. Satisfied that the grateful monarch would follow his instructions, he bid the town farewell and moved on.

THE GOLDEN LEGEND

THE LEGEND of St George's chivalrous act appeared in writing from the twelfth century but it was the *Golden Legend*, written around 1260 by Jacobus de Voragine, which popularised the story. This compilation of the 'real lives' of over a hundred saints was a medieval best-seller. Over 900 lengthy manuscripts survive today and, when printing was introduced, it became the most often reproduced book in Europe from 1470 to 1530. In 1483 Kent-born print pioneer William Caxton published the first English translation of the *Golden Legend*. Voragine's stories are often fanciful and even he had to admit they should be taken with a large dose of salt. Twentieth-century translator William Granger Ryan has the author advising that the story of St Margaret of Antioch being swallowed by a dragon was 'apocryphal and not to be taken seriously'.

Dragons feature heavily in the tales and St George is by no means the only saint to have vanquished the beast. As well as St Margaret, who apparently dissolved the evil creature from within, St Martha was said to have slain 'a great dragon, half beast and half fish, greater than an ox, longer than an horse, having teeth sharp as a sword, and horned on either side, head like a lion, tail like a serpent, and defended him with two wings on either side, and could not be beaten with cast of stones ne [*sic*] with other armour, and was as strong as twelve lions or bears'. After finding him in the woods, close to the River Rhone, Martha 'cast on him holy water, and showed to him the cross, which anon was overcome, and standing still as a sheep, she bound him with her own girdle, and then was slain with spears and glaives of the people. The dragon was called of them that dwelled in the country.'

Another little-known saint who used the power of God against a man-eating creature was St Silvester, who was visited by St Peter and given the power to overcome. The following is an extract from William Caxton's 1483 translation.

In this time it happed that there was at Rome a dragon in a pit, which every day slew with his breath more than three hundred men. Then came the bishops of the idols unto the emperor and said unto him: 'O thou most holy emperor, sith the time that thou hast received Christian faith the dragon which is in yonder fosse or pit slayeth every day with his breath more than three hundred men.' Then sent the emperor for S. Silvester and asked counsel of him of this matter. S. Silvester answered that by the might of God he promised to make him cease of his hurt and blessure of this people. Then S. Silvester put himself to prayer, and S. Peter appeared to him and said: 'Go surely to the dragon and the two priests that be with thee take in thy company, and when thou shalt come to him thou shalt say to him in this manner: Our Lord Jesu Christ which was born of the Virgin Mary, crucified, buried and arose, and now sitteth on the right side of the Father, this is he that shall come to deem and judge the living and the dead, I commend thee Sathanas that thou abide him in this place till he come. Then thou shalt bind his mouth with a thread, and seal it with thy seal, wherein is the imprint of the cross. Then thou and the two priests shall come to me whole and safe, and such bread as I shall make ready for you ye shall eat.'

Thus as S. Peter had said, S. Silvester did. And when he came to the pit, he descended down one hundred and fifty steps, bearing with him two lanterns, and found the dragon, and said the words that S. Peter had said to him, and bound his mouth with the thread, and sealed it, and after returned, and as he came upward again he met with two enchanters which followed him for to see if he descended, which were almost dead of the stench of the dragon, whom he brought with him whole and sound, which anon were baptised, with a great multitude of people with them. Thus was the city of Rome delivered from double death, that was from the culture and worshipping of false idols, and from the venom of the dragon.

DRAGONS – SUPERSTITION
AND SYMBOLISM

ANY OF THOSE listening to St George's tale in medieval times would have believed the battle to be real and his foe an actual creature. To a modern reader it may seem incredible that the tale would be taken literally, but in medieval society belief in dragons was widespread. Much of the world and many of its indigenous creatures lay undiscovered, and for ordinary mortals travel was rare. The intrepid few who ventured far and wide returned with tales of scaly monsters – most likely to have been large crocodiles – and there were even some unexplained dragon sightings documented in England itself. In 1233, during a time of civil unrest in the reign of Henry III, two dragons were reportedly seen fighting off the south coast and in 1395 another fearsome creature was said to have terrorised parts of the country. The men and cattle around St Leonard's Forest, near Horsham, apparently fell victim in the mid-seventeenth century, and as late as 1725 Newcastle curate Henry Bourne wrote that the bonfires traditionally lit on Midsummer Eve were to drive dragons away. The creatures, he said, 'incited to lust through the heat of the season did frequently, as they flew through the air, spermatize in the wells and fountains'.[1]

In the *Golden Legend* the dragon in a saint's story is almost always a symbol of evil, of dark and, more specifically, a representation of the devil. Satan appears in the guise of a dragon in many a myth, most notably those of St Michael and St Margaret.

In the passage on Archangel Michael, Voragine wrote,

> For like as Daniel witnesseth, he shall arise and address in
> the time of Antichrist against him, and shall stand as a
> defender and keeper for them that be chosen. He also fought
> with the dragon and his angels, and casting them out of
> heaven, had a great victory. He also had a great plea and
> altercation with the devil for the body of Moses, because he
> would not show it; for the children of Israel should have
> adored and worshipped it.

As Margaret of Antioch is held in a prison she asks God to reveal her enemy.

> And whilst she was in prison, she prayed our Lord that the
> fiend that had fought with her, he would visibly show him
> unto her. And then appeared a horrible dragon and assailed
> her, and would have devoured her, but she made the sign of
> the cross, and anon he vanished away. And in another place it

1. Samantha Riches, *St George: Hero, Martyr and Myth.*

is said that he swallowed her into his belly, she making the sign of the Cross. And the belly brake asunder, and so she issued out all whole and sound.

Earlier tellers of the life and martyrdom of St George, such as Aelfric, make no mention of the dragon-slaying myth, which would suggest that Voragine inserted the episode as an illustration of our hero's bravery and purity in the face of evil.

THE BATTLEGROUND

DESPITE THE *Golden Legend's* clear and specific mention of the town of Silene in Libya, there are several places across Europe that claim the epic battle as their own. In Britain, Dragon Hill in Berkshire boasts a bare patch of chalk which is said to have been caused by the spilling of the beast's blood, poisoning the ground so that no grass could grow there. The theory was mentioned in the writings of the Reverend Francis Wise in 1738, and it was thought that the nearby White Horse of Uffington, the famous chalk landmark, actually represented the dragon itself. Other places to claim the victory include St George in Wales and Brinsop in Herefordshire, where the church once welcomed the congregation with a Norman tympanum (carving above the door) of the saint slaughtering the dragon, which has now been moved inside. The dragon is seen as a wingless serpent with a grotesque head while George is depicted as a Roman soldier, spearing the creature in the mouth.

Many of the British-based legends seem to err towards the version found in Richard Johnson's sixteenth-century book *The Most Famous History of the Seven Champions of Christendom*. In this retelling George was actually from Coventry and killed the dragon in order to save the beautiful daughter of the sultan of Egypt, thus winning her hand in marriage. The happy couple then went on to have three children, one of whom was the legendary Guy of Warwick, famed as something of a dab hand at monster-slaying himself, having dispatched the evil Dun Cow at Dunsmore Heath. This massive creature belonged to a giant in Shropshire and dispensed an inexhaustible supply of milk. But when an old lady attempted to fill her sieve as well as her bucket, the cow broke loose and wandered to Dunsmore Heath where she was killed by Sir Guy. Her huge horn, which may in fact be an elephant's tusk, is in Warwick Castle to this day.

> On Dunsmore Heath I alsoe stewe
> A monstrous wyld and cruell beast,
> Calld the Dun-Cow of Dunsmore Heath;
> Which many people had opprest.

Some of her bones in Warwick yett

Still for a monument doe lye.[2]

In *British Dragons*, author Jacqueline Simpson identifies fifty-eight places in the UK with dragon legends attached although most have no direct link with St George. However, the Johnson version of the legend has George fighting a second dragon, which was wreaking havoc in an English town, and this time perishing in the battle rather than the widely accepted martyrdom.

JACOBUS DE VORAGINE

JACOBUS DE VORAGINE was born in Voragine, now Varazze, in Italy in 1230. Having entered the Dominican order in 1244, he became a professor at the age of twenty-two and used his great skills as an orator to preach throughout Italy. Impressing his superiors with his devotion and piety, he quickly rose through the ranks of the order. In 1267, he was awarded the title of provincial superior (a kind of regional supervisor) in Lombardy, the region with Milan as its capital. He held this post for nearly twenty years before being removed

2. Thomas Percy, *Reliques of Ancient English Poetry*, 'The Legend of Sir Guy', 1765.

after a meeting of Dominican leaders in Paris. He attended the councils of Lucca and Ferrara and was instrumental in Pope Nicolas IV's bid to depose the order's master Munio de Zamora in 1291. Shortly afterwards, Jacobus was made archbishop of Genoa, where he mediated in the deadly rivalry between the Guelfs and the Ghibellines.

During his lifetime he wrote many works, a fact he himself pointed out in his *Chronicon januense* (*Chronicle of Genoa*): 'While he was in his order, and after he had been made archbishop, he wrote many works. For he compiled the legends of the saints in one volume, adding many things from the *Historia tripartita et scholastica*, and from the chronicles of many writers.' He also claimed to have written several anonymous volumes of sermons and a weighty tome on the holy figure of the Virgin Mary.

He died in 1298 or 1299, and was buried under the main altar in the Dominican church at Genoa. In 1816, he was beatified by Pope Pius VII.

THE VIRGIN

MUCH IS MADE of the princess's unmarried status in the *Golden Legend*. In fact her distraught father's first thought is that he will not see her wed. 'When the king saw he might no more do, he began to weep, and said to his daughter: Now shall I never see thine espousals.' When he finally concedes he has no choice but to sacrifice her, he dresses her in a wedding dress to meet her fate. 'Then did the king do array his daughter like as she should be wedded, and embraced her, kissed her and gave her his benediction, and after, led her to the place where the dragon was.'

The king's despair that he will never see his daughter wed is significant in that it indicates her virginity and innocence. If the dragon is Satan or a manifestation of evil, then the intended victim's purity makes his crime all the more heinous and the hero's intervention even more necessary.

The fact that the lady is a virgin is also pertinent to the legend of St George because of his close ties to the Virgin Mary. Frequently referred to as Our Lady's knight in English hymns, the saint is often pictured alongside the Virgin in art-work from the thirteenth century onwards, and many images show the saint being resurrected by the Virgin's hand. The

Golden Legend itself makes reference to the knight's allegiance to Mary, saying, 'The king did do make a church there of our Lady and of S. George, in the which yet sourdeth a fountain of living water, which healeth sick people that drink thereof.'

Other interpretations can be put on the chaste status of the damsel in the dragon tale. In Swedish myth, for example, the princess has come to represent the innocence of Sweden, while the dragon is seen as an invading army with St George as the country's Holy protector.

CHAPTER TWO

The Man and the Martyr

T HE TRUE IDENTITY and origins of St George are mysteries that have puzzled many an academic in the past, and no definitive conclusion has yet been reached. However, the bulk of expert opinion has settled on a Christian martyr born in central Turkey and martyred on 23 April 303. Various other regions have claimed his birthplace, including Armorica, a region of modern-day France, the Palestinian town of Lydda, where he was later martyred, and even Coventry. The most widely accepted birthplace, however, is Cappadocia, mentioned in the *Golden Legend* and linked to the saint in many retellings of his story by the often used title St George of Cappadocia.

The issue of his birthplace is somewhat clouded by another less savoury fourth-century figure known as George of Cappadocia (or Laodicaea). Although archbishop of Alexandria, he was a corrupt and immoral figure who was said to have amassed a fortune collecting taxes and selling dodgy meat to the army. According to C S Huist's 1910 book *St George of Cappadocia in Legend and History*, this George was part of the Arian heresy, a religious sect which believed that Jesus was no more than a mortal being. As such, he persecuted orthodox Christians until a rebellion around 358 caused him to flee for his life. When he regained his position through military intervention, he carried on with his persecution until finally the new Roman emperor, Julian, sentenced him to prison. The punishment proved too light for the angry Alexandrians, who dragged him from his cell in 362, killed him and threw his body into the sea.

In *The Decline and Fall of the Roman Empire* the eighteenth-century historian Edward Gibbon asserted that the heretic George was one and the same as St George the Christian martyr. Subsequent study of dates, placenames and methods of death in the two stories has led to this theory being largely dismissed.

The 'real' St George, it is believed, was born around 270 to Roman Christian parents who held lofty positions in society. Early Coptic (or Egyptian) texts name his father as Anastasius, governor of Militene in Cappadocia, and his grandfather John governor of the province. His mother is given as Kîra Theognôsta, daughter of Dionysus, count of Lydda. Samantha Riches, author of *St George: Hero, Martyr and Myth*, comments that this provenance is 'a neat device that allows the two main sites claiming St George to be given similar weighting.' She goes on to say that Kîra was said to have links with the saints 'that dwelt at Lydda' and even to Joseph of Arimathea. 'Linking pseudo-historical saints with "real" Biblical characters was a common medieval device aimed at substantiating the claims of sanctity of otherwise dubious figures.'

Manuscripts found during 1964 excavations of the Byzantine Qasr Ibrim cathedral in Upper Egypt tell a different story, attributing the baby George to a Christian mother, Polychronia, who baptised her son against her husband's wishes. However, further evidence that both parents were Christian appeared in a fifth-century manuscript purporting to have been written by a servant of the saint, a man called Pasicrates who claimed to have witnessed his torture and death. This character may well have been invented by early Christian writers in a bid to authenticate the saint's story.

Most accounts claim that George was a soldier, or knight, in the imperial army in Palestine, which was part of the Roman empire at the turn of the fourth century. The *Passion of St George*, written by Ælfric, archbishop of York, and published in 1000, states, 'The holy Georius was in heathenish days a rich earldorman under the fierce Caesar Datianus, In the shire of Cappodocia.' Seeking further promotion, legend has it, he travelled to the Palestinian town of Diospolis, later known as Lydda, the area most commonly associated with his martyrdom.

That a Christian should be so favoured in the imperial army, where worship of the traditional Roman gods was the accepted religion, may seem strange, but at the start of the reign of Emperor Diocletian, ruler between 284 and 305, Christianity was universally tolerated. It was not until around 299, after reports of disobedience in the ranks and suspected plots among the Christians, that Diocletian began to persecute those who refused to denounce their faith. One popular story has it that the pagan emperor made a sacrifice to the gods and then called in the augurs, or priests, to read the entrails, as was customary. The augurs told him they could not predict the future from the animal organs because of hostility from Christians within the imperial household. Diocletian then issued an edict forcing members of his household to make sacrifices to the gods and also sent a letter to the army chiefs demanding the same of soldiers. Those refusing to denounce their Christian faith were dismissed and in many cases tortured and killed.

According to the *Golden Legend* some 22,000 Christian men were martyred in just one month. St George, the legend says, shed 'the habit of a knight' and gave all his worldly goods away to the poor before taking up a life of preaching to the pagans and declaring, 'All the gods of the paynims [heathens] and gentiles be devils, my God made the heavens and is very God.' A provost, named by Voragine as Dacian, challenged the brave preacher and asked who he was. 'He answered anon and said: I am named George, I am a gentleman, a knight of Cappadocia, and have left all for to serve the God of heaven.' Refusing to denounce his faith, George was horribly tortured by the provost, who

> did do raise him on a gibbet; and so much beat him with
> great staves and broches of iron, that his body was all to
> broken in pieces. And after he did do take brands of iron and
> join them to his sides, and his bowels which then appeared he
> did do frot with salt, and so sent him into prison, but our
> Lord appeared to him of the same night with great light and
> comforted him much sweetly. And by this great consolation
> he took to him so good heart that he doubted no torment
> that they might make him suffer.

In William Granger Ryan's translation of the *Golden Legend* the official 'commanded that he be stretched on the rack and had him torn, limb from limb, with hooks. His body was burned with burning torches and salt was rubbed into his gaping wounds.'

When these trials failed to weaken George's resolve, the frustrated provost called his magician, usually named as Athanasius, who mixed a powerful poison and added it to wine under the threat of decapitation if it did not have the desired effect. Having made the sign of the Cross over the cup, George drank every drop and was unaffected. Athanasius then repeated the exercise with stronger venom and, when George remained standing, was so impressed that he converted to Christianity, kneeling before his intended victim to beg forgiveness. As soon as Dacian learned of his magician's betrayal, he cut off his head.

The following day George was 'bound upon a wheel that was fitted with sharp knives, but the wheel fell apart at once and the saint remained unharmed'. Dacian then had the saint thrown into a vat of molten lead, 'but George made the sign of the Cross and, by God's power, settled down as though he were in a refreshing bath.'

Seeing the torture was having no effect, the provost attempted to win George over with 'fair words', telling him that the gods would soon run out of patience and begging him to make a sacrifice and be rewarded with great honours. 'Why did you not say this at the beginning?' replied George. 'I am ready to do as you say.' Thrilled, Dacian told the whole town that the persecuted man had given in and asked them to gather to watch him make his sacrifice at the temple. But when George knelt in worship with the assembled crowd waiting to hear the dedication to the pagan deities, he prayed instead to his own god and asked him to destroy the temple and convert the people. 'And anon the fire descended from heaven and burnt the temple, and the idols, and their priests, and the earth opened and swallowed all the cinders and ashes that were left.'

Dacian was furious, having the saint dragged before him and asking, 'What evil deeds have you done? You are the wickedest of men.' George retorted that the provost should not believe what he had not seen and should come along in person to watch him make a sacrifice. Dacian refused, calling George a fraud and declaring, 'thou wilt make the earth to swallow me, like as thou hast the temple and my gods'.

'How can your gods, who could not help themselves, help you?' asked his prisoner.

Defeated once more, Dacian turned to his wife, Alexandria, and told her, 'I shall die for anger if I may not surmount and overcome this man.'

'Evil and cruel tyrant!' she replied. 'Can you not see the great virtue of the Christian people? I told you not to harm them because their God fights for them well. Now I shall become a Christian too.' Dacian was angry, took her by the hair, and beat and tortured her. 'What will become of me?' she asked the suffering saint. 'I am not baptised.'

'Fear not,' he answered. 'You will be baptised in your own blood.' As she was put to death, she prayed to Jesus Christ.

The next day Dacian ordered that George be dragged through the city and beheaded. Before his death he prayed to the Lord that all those who asked for his help would be granted it, and a voice from heaven assured him this would be so. On 23 April, in the year 303 his head was cut off and the martyr legend was born.

Dacian paid for his bloodthirsty ways. As he returned home from the execution, fire rained down from the heavens and consumed him and his entourage.

OTHER THEORIES

WHILE THE bare bones of the martyrdom story remain fairly consistent throughout the retellings, there are some variants in the detail.

Even in the *Golden Legend*, Voragine admitted that the reports were sketchy, particularly when it came to the city of George's death and the identity of his persecutor.

> And his legend is numbered among other scriptures apocryphal in the council of Nicene, because his martyrdom hath no certain relation. For in the calendar of Bede it is said that he suffered martyrdom in Persia in the city of Diaspolin, and in other places it is read that he resteth in the city of Diaspolin which tofore was called Lidda, which is by the city of Joppa or Japh. And in another place it is said that he suffered death under Diocletian and Maximian, which that time were emperors. And in another place under Diocletian emperor of Persia, being present seventy kings of his empire. And it is said here that he suffered death under Dacian the provost, then Diocletian and Maximian being emperors.

Other accounts have linked him to incidents of rebellion in Nicomedia, now known as Izmit, in north-west Turkey. In

322 Eusebius, bishop of Caesarea, wrote that when a decree outlawing Christianity and demanding those who practise it submit to slavery was posted, a 'man of great distinction' tore it down and publicly destroyed it. For this, the Emperor Diocletian sentenced him to death. After lengthy tortures, during which he showed unfailing courage, he was executed on 23 April 303. While some believe the unnamed man was St Nestor, others claim that this was the real St George.

The methods of torture also vary from tale to tale. Ælfric, in 1000, made no mention of the rack but said the saint was 'scourged', a common Roman practice which involved being beaten with a short leather whip called a *flagrum*, consisting of leather thongs knotted around sheep bones on iron balls. The *Golden Legend* also added knives to the wheel of torture mentioned in Ælfric. *Mirk's Festial*, a collection of sermons from the Augustine author John Mirk published around 1403, included a 'mylne-ston vpon his brest, forto haue so cruschet hym to dep'[3] and a 'bote brennyng lyme-kylne'[4] in which he was baked overnight and came out alive when all other men would have been burnt to ashes. Carmelite author Baptista Spagnuoli Mantuanus, known as the Mantuan, added the dragging of St George through the streets behind a team of bulls; and various other tortures, including being nailed to a table, being made to wear spiked shoes and being burned on a pyre, have

3. 'millstone upon his breast to crush him to death'
4. 'burning lime kiln'

appeared in literary and pictorial accounts of his ordeal. Some stories claim the torture stretched up to seven years, and that his constant resurrection from certain death led to many thousands of conversions to Christianity.

RELICS

ACCORDING TO the sixth-century religious historian Gregory of Tours, the remains of St George were taken away to an unknown burial place by some Christian devotees. On their way they rested in an oratory in a hospital, and the following morning found they could not open the door to leave until they had left some of the saint's relics behind. An account mentioned in the *Golden Legend* names the site of his entombment as a town called Ramys, situated between Jerusalem and Jaffa. There, according to Caxton's translation, 'is a chapel of S. George which is now desolate and uncovered, and therein dwell Christian Greeks. And in the said chapel lieth the body of S. George, but not the head. And there lie his father and mother and his uncle, not in the chapel but under the wall of the chapel.'

In medieval times much was made of the relics or remains of saints, said to bring miracles to those who saw or touched them, and George's various body parts appear to have been scattered all over Europe and the Middle East. In the year 751 Pope Zacharias discovered St George's head in Rome – this ended up in the city of Ferrara. A different head was kept in a church in Reichenau in Germany, a third in Syria and a fourth rescued from Constantinople in 1453, after the city fell to the Turks. A head with a helmet was presented to St George's Chapel at Windsor Castle by Edward IV. In 1971 a further skull was discovered in an abbey on St George's Island in Venice. Clearly the saint didn't have six heads, but, as Sam Riches observes, 'the proliferation of body parts of saints was apparently an accepted part of belief at this time'.

Throughout history, kings of England have believed they held relics of the country's patron saint. Edward III owned a vial of blood, included in an inventory in 1331, and Henry VII's last will and testament mentioned a section of St George's leg, a gift from his cousin Louis of France.

CHAPTER THREE

Worldwide Icon

EORGE HAS LONG been associated with England but his influence spreads considerably wider. The country of Georgia, a former Soviet state which gained independence in 1991, is named in his honour, and its flag is a large St George's cross with a smaller red cross in each of the four white sections. Its coat of arms shows the knight on horseback, slaying the dragon with a long spear. In the eighteenth century Georgian prince and geographer Vakhushti Bagrationi reported that his country had 365 churches devoted to the saint, one for each day of the year.

George is also the patron saint of Aragon, Catalonia, Lithuania, Palestine and Malta. In the reign of King John I (1357–1433), St George became the patron saint of Portugal and it was decreed that the saint's image would be carried on the Catholic feast day of Corpus Christi.

In the Russian Orthodox Church St George is venerated as the great martyr George the Trophy Bearer and 'St George for Holy Russia' was once the battle cry of the tsars. In fact despite the written account of George's battle with the dragon appearing some time later, the image of the saint slaying the beast was incorporated into the arms of Moscow as early as the ninth century. The coat of arms of Princess Anne of Kiev, who married King Henry I of France in 1051, depicts the dragon legend, and it also appears in an image in St George's church in Kiev carved at the beginning of the tenth century. In the Ukraine he has been revered since Christianity was established in 988 by Volodymyr the Great, and in Prague a Romanesque monastic order established St George's church in the castle in 920.

The French region of Normandy has strong associations with the saint, and in the medieval period boasted seventy churches and two healing springs in his name as well as four sites which claimed to hold relics. Although there was a connection with England for hundreds of years after the conquest of that country by the Normans in 1066, it seems the locals had been venerating him since the sixth century. The strength of feeling grew when a coffer containing relics and a manuscript of the Gospels in Latin, along with a fragment believed to be of Jesus Christ's actual cross, was washed up on the shores of Cotentin. One of the relics was thought to be St George's jawbone. Local leaders, stunned by this discovery, decided that only God could choose what should be done with the relics, so they put them onto a cart pulled by oxen, and let the animals wander where they would. Where they came to a rest, at the hilltop village of Brix, a church was built to honour St George along with two further sanctuaries, dedicated to the Virgin Mary and the Holy Cross.

Ironically, William of Normandy, called the Conqueror, is reported to have flown the standard of the red cross of St George from the masthead of his ship when he arrived to defeat the Anglo-Saxons at the Battle of Hastings.

INTERNATIONAL CUSTOMS

✠ In Catalonia, *La Diada de Sant Jordi* marks the second most important feast in the calendar and tradition has it that a book and a rose should be given to a loved one. William Shakespeare was born and died on 23 April, and Spanish author Miguel de Cervantes also died that day (in the Gregorian calendar). In 1995 these three facts inspired UNESCO to name St George's Day International Book Day.

✠ In Belgium, in the city of Mons, the battle between George and the dragon is re-enacted each year by forty-six players in a show known as *Combat dit Lumeçon* watched by crowds of thousands. If a spectator can grab a piece of the dragon they will have a year's good luck.

✝ In Bulgaria, St George's Day or *Gergyovden* is one of the most important feasts in the calendar. As in many countries, it falls on 6 May, as the Orthodox Church uses the Julian calendar rather than the Gregorian, and in Bulgaria it is a public holiday. The occasion is marked by the cooking and eating of a whole lamb, which honours the martyr's position as patron saint of shepherds. Thanks to St George's links to the military, this date was also declared Bulgarian Army Day in 1880, and is marked with impressive parades in the capital, Sofia.

✝ In Serbia and Montenegro, as well as other Serbian lands, the feast falls on 6 May and is known as Đurđevdan. It is an important day for families and is generally celebrated with picnics, folk dancing and music. In many eastern European countries the date is also celebrated as *Ederlezi*, a celebration of spring and a traditional feast day for Romani Gypsies.

✝ In Turkey, *Hidirellez* or *Hidrellez* is celebrated on 6 May to mark the day when al-Khidr, believed to be the Muslim equivalent of St George, met the prophet Elijah on earth.

✝ The Palestinian city of Bethlehem sees the feast celebrated by both Muslims and Christians, who hang pictures of the saint over their front doors to ward off evil. West of the city, in a town called al-Khader in his honour, is a monastery devoted to him and near Jericho is another. In Beit Jala stands an interfaith shrine also visited by Jews, who believe it is the burial place of Elijah. In 1866 Elizabeth Finn, the wife of the British consul in Jerusalem, wrote, 'St George killed the dragon in this country Palestine; and the place is shown close to Beyrut. Many churches and convents are named after him. The church at Lydda is dedicated to St George: so is a convent near Bethlehem, and another small one just opposite the Jaffa gate; and others beside.' Scottish travel writer William Dalrymple travelled to the shrine in 1995 and recorded his impressions in his book *From the Holy Mountain: a journey among the Christians of the Middle East.*

> I asked around in the Christian Quarter in Jerusalem, and
> discovered that the pace was very much alive. With all the
> greatest shrines in the Christian world to choose from, it
> seemed that when the local Arab Christians had a problem –
> an illness, or something more complicated: a husband detained
> in an Israeli prison camp, for example – they preferred to seek
> the intercession of St George in his grubby little shrine at Beit
> Jala rather than praying at the Holy Sepulchre in Jerusalem or
> the Church of the Nativity in Bethlehem.

He also asked the priest at the shrine whether many Muslims attended. The priest replied, 'We get hundreds! Almost as many as the Christian pilgrims. Often, when I come in here, I find Muslims all over the floor, in the aisles, up and down.'

✝ The Russian Orthodox Church celebrates the saint's day twice a year. The first is on the traditional date of 6 May

(Julian calendar) and the second on 26 November (9 December in the Gregorian calendar), the anniversary of Yarslav I's dedication of the church of St George in Kiev. The days are named *Vesenniy Yuriev Den* (Yuri's Day in the Spring) and *Osenniy Yuriev Den* (Yuri's Day in the Autumn).

✝ The Brazilian people have inherited their love of the saint from Portugal, whose flag flew over the country until the nineteenth century. He is especially revered in Rio de Janeiro, where his feast day is as important as that of the city's patron St Sebastian. In São Paulo, he is the patron saint of the local football club, Corinthians, whose home ground is called Parque São Jorge. Brazil has the biggest catholic population in the world, and St George is the most popular saint. Many people use his name as an exclamation, saying 'My St George from Capadoccia' as a Brit would say 'Oh my God!'

✝ India has many churches dedicated to St George, particularly in the state of Kerala. On 6 and 7 May, many pilgrims make their way to the village of Puthupally, to the sixteenth-century Malankara Orthodox church, or to the St George Pilgrimage centre at Puthiyathura. Celebrations in some parts of Kerala can last up to ten days. Local belief has it that the saint was the brother of the goddess Kali, and George, or various derivations of it, is the most popular Christian baptismal name in the region.

FASCINATING FACT

Fans of the Sacha Baron Cohen movie *Borat: Cultural Learnings of America for Make Benefit Glorious Nation of Kazakhstan* may recognise a folk song entitled '*Ederlezi (Scena Djurdjevdana Na Rijeci)*', which translates as '*Ederlezi* (Scene of St George's Day on the River)'. In fact, this song has no connection to Kazakhstan but is a feast-day folk song which evolved from a traditional Balkan Romani song for the Muslim festival of *Ederlezi*, which celebrates the arrival of spring. As this also falls on 6 May, the Balkan Slavs added the Christian chorus:

Hey, here comes the dawn, here comes the dawn
To pray to God
Here comes the dawn, here comes the dawn
Hey, it's St George's Day
And I'm not with the one I love
Let her name be mentioned
On every other day
On every other day
Except on St George's Day

In fact, there is no river scene in the Borat film; instead, the title of the song was lifted from the soundtrack of the 1988 movie *Time of the Gypsies* from Serbian director Emir Kusturica, which did feature a river celebration.

GEORGE AND GEORGIA

FOLK STORIES about St George are common in his name-sake country of Georgia, and the following tale demonstrates how highly he is regarded among the farmers and shepherds of the country, often being revered more than Jesus himself.

Once St George was travelling through Georgia with Jesus and the prophet Elias, and became tired and hungry. Seeing a Georgian shepherd they decided to stop and ask for food. Elias approached the man and asked him for a sheep. The shepherd asked who he was and Elias answered, 'I am the one who sends rain to help the crops grow so you make a good profit from your farm.' But the shepherd grew angry and said, 'But you also send thunderstorms, which destroy the farms of poor widows.'

Next, Jesus spoke to the man and asked for a sheep, explaining, 'I am God, the creator of all things.' Once again the shepherd was angry, saying, 'Then you also take away the souls of good young men and grant dishonest men long lives.'

Finally, St George approached the shepherd and asked if he could spare a sheep.

'And who are you?' asked the man. 'I am St George,' came

the reply, 'on whom you call when you are troubled and who protects you from evil.'

The shepherd immediately dropped to his knees in reverence and gave him everything he owned.

THE ALFA ROMEO MYTH

THE ICONIC Alfa Romeo badge, with a white cross on one side and a serpent on the other, is falsely believed by some to allude to the story of St George and the dragon. In fact, it is based on the coat of arms of the Visconti family and refers to two different legends. The first, from the car manufacturer's home city of Milan, is the tale of a fierce man-eating serpent in the fifth century, who terrified the inhabitants and was heroically slain by Ottoni Visconti. The second has a connection to St George in that it reputedly celebrates the life of crusader Giovanni da Rio, who was said to be the first to climb the walls of Jerusalem and erect a cross during the First Crusade. A red cross against a white background is also the flag of Milan, and is thought to come from the colours of St Ambrose, the city's patron. The original badge was designed by Romano Cattaneo in 1910.

CHAPTER FOUR

Soldier Saint

Now order the ranks, and fling wide the banners, for
our souls are God's and our bodies the king's, and our
swords for St George and for England!

SIR ARTHUR CONAN DOYLE, *The White Company*

ST GEORGE has long been associated with military campaigns and is seen as the patron saint of soldiers. It is believed he was an officer in the imperial Roman army, having enlisted in its cavalry at the age of seventeen during the reign of the skilled military tactician Diocletian. Tall and handsome, he was noted among his peers for his military bearing, his valour and strength, and was promoted to the rank of tribune, roughly equivalent to a colonel, the leader of some 1,000 men.

In the dragon legend he is presented as a fearless knight and defender of the innocent, and it is in this guise that he is often painted, with a white tunic bearing a red cross over chain mail or plate armour. Many a battle cry has been yelled in his name, and if stories of returning warriors are to believed, it is

St George's habit to appear on the battlefield in times of need to guide the 'righteous' army to victory.

His first ghostly appearance was not to aid an English army but a Norman one. In 1063 the Normans were vastly outnumbered by a Saracen army at Cerami in Sicily, but the saintly apparition gained them another victory. The cult of St George arrived with them when they defeated King Harold at the Battle of Hastings in 1066 and English devotion was heightened by fantastic stories brought back by the knights of the crusades during the eleventh and twelfth centuries.

KNIGHT OF THE CRUSADES

WILLIAM THE CONQUEROR's eldest son Robert, duke of Normandy, adopted St George as his patron saint when he set off for the First Crusade in 1095, and three years later the saint was on hand to guide the Christian soldiers to an important strategic victory at Antioch, modern-day Antakya in Turkey. The city of Antioch was of huge significance to the crusaders due to its links to early Christianity. Its citizens were among the first to be converted to the new faith after hearing Peter himself preach there and were the first to be termed

'Christians'. It also had great strategic value, being close to the coast and the port of St Symeon.

In 1097 and 1098 the population was still largely Christian but the city had fallen under the rule of Turkish Muslims. The crusaders, mainly made up of small French and Norman contingents under the leadership of different nobles, arrived in the autumn after an arduous journey and laid siege to the city. Defended by a long wall, the sprawling city was fairly self-sufficient and would not easily be starved out. Crusader morale was low. The men were exhausted, low on supplies and in some cases on the verge of starvation themselves. Their leaders couldn't decide the best way to take the city and arguments broke out between the different factions.

Eventually, the crusaders had a stroke of luck when a traitor from within the city let down a ladder so that several knights could climb in and open the gates. The Turks were slaughtered and the Antioch Christians murdered the governor. But the crusaders were about to face more trouble, in the shape of a large Turkish army which had been mobilised to relieve the besieged city and was advancing fast. Many of the terrified crusaders fled the city and those left behind were ravished with hunger and disease. The intimidated Byzantine emperor reneged on his promise of help, and morale sank further.

The situation was saved by a peasant known as Peter Bartholomew, who came to the crusaders claiming to have seen St Andrew, who had told him the whereabouts of the Holy

Lance, the actual weapon that had pierced the flesh of Jesus Christ at his crucifixion. The soldiers set about searching for the spear in the city's church of St Peter and eventually it was 'miraculously' uncovered by the peasant himself. He then told the battle-fatigued men that their fallen comrades and all the saints would fight alongside them, and amazingly the reinvigorated crusaders opted to fast in the days ahead as they prayed to God to help them on the battlefield.

When the Muslim army approached, the priests and nobles urged the starving crusaders to throw open the gates and charge out, carrying the Holy Lance before them. But, according to legend, the Turkish army never reached them, attacked first by a ghostly army fronted by St George. With St Maurice, St Demetrius and St Theodore by his side, the soldier saint was said to have led an entire regiment of dead crusaders holding white banners against the advancing Turks, who turned and fled before the incredulous eyes of the Christians.

The Caxton translation of the *Golden Legend* records a similar event at the crusaders' next port of call, the holy city of Jerusalem, in 1099. 'It is also found in the history of Antioch, that when the Christian men went over sea to conquer Jerusalem, that one, a right fair young man, appeared to a priest of the host and counselled him that he should bear with him a little of the relics of St George, for he was conductor of the battle, and so he did so much that he had some.'

The city was of huge significance, being the site of Christ's crucifixion, and also contained his supposed burial place, under the church of the Holy Sepulchre. But it was also holy to Muslims and, unlike Antioch, contained no Christian inhabitants to aid the crusaders once they breached the walls. The Christians besieged the town but an initial assault failed. Then a priest claimed that a vision had told him they must march barefoot around the walls, repenting of their sins. The 15,000 men, led by priests bearing the Holy Lance and a reliquary containing St George's arm bone, did just that. English and Italian ships also arrived with reinforcements and much-needed supplies, giving a huge boost to morale. Siege towers were built, and in the next assault crusaders flooded across the battlements, opened the city gates to let more in and the Christians once more tasted victory. Many claimed that what really changed the course of events was the sight of St George, dressed in white armour adorned with the red cross, leading an army over the city walls. 'They saw appertly [*sic*] St George which had white arms with a red cross, that went up tofore them on the walls, and they followed him, and so was Jerusalem taken by his help.'

RICHARD THE LIONHEART

CRUSADING KING Richard I spent less than six months of his ten-year reign in England, having been crowned in 1189 and set off almost immediately to 'fight the good fight'. Two years before his coronation Jerusalem had fallen to the Muslims under warrior leader Saladin. In response, European monarchs including Frederick Barbarossa of Germany, Philip II of France and Richard pooled their resources in a bid to reclaim the city. The Third Crusade was under way.

Key to the campaign's success was the capture of the Palestinian port city of Acre. From 1189, a fifteen-month stand-off had existed between the Christian soldiers and the city's Muslim defenders, but in the summer of 1191, 8,000 English crusaders arrived in a hundred ships to join the armies of Philip of France and Leopold of Austria, and the combined troops were able to seal off the city. After a planned meeting with Saladin fell through, due to the kings of England and France falling ill, the crusaders attacked the walls with specially constructed machines. Before they began, however, Richard was said to have seen a vision of St George, which spurred him on. The news of this apparition had a profound effect on the weary men, just as a century before it had boosted morale in Antioch and Jerusalem.

On 12 July, the city surrendered. After negotiations over the release of prisoners broke down, warrior of Christ Richard the Lionheart had thousands of Muslims decapitated.

Following his victories Richard is said to have rebuilt the tomb at Lydda destroyed by Saladin where St George's remains were thought to be housed, but there is little evidence to support this. In fact, despite the story of St George's appearance at Acre, Richard may not have had any great allegiance to the saint and does not appear to have fought under his banner. Instead, it was, Edward I who was the first recorded English king to fly the arms of St George in battle, during his 1277 war with the Welsh.

THE KNIGHTS TEMPLAR

THIS ORDER OF holy knights, made notorious by the recent novels of Dan Brown, had strong connections to England's patron saint. Formed between 1118 and 1120, the order began as nine pious knights whose original purpose was to protect pilgrims travelling through the Holy Land. Led by Hugh de Payens, they offered their services to the Christian king of Jerusalem Baldwin II, and were granted a wing of the royal palace on the Temple Mount.

Members of the order initially lived like monks and wore white mantles if they were knights, black for sergeants. However, in 1143, members were permitted to add a red cross to their outfits, signifying a link to the gallant knight St George.

Carvings at the long-hidden Royston Cave in Hertfordshire show the order revered four saints in particular – St Christopher, patron saint of travellers; St Lawrence, who was martyred after rescuing the Holy Grail; St Catherine, later connected to the Templars by a victory over the Saracens on St Catherine's Day 1177; and our own St George. The cave, rediscovered by a workman in 1742, was thought to be a meeting place for the Templars during their persecution by Philip IV of France and Pope Clement V in the early fourteenth century. The wall carvings show all four saints as well as mysterious symbols and pictures thought by some to denote the birth of a son of Jesus to Mary Magdalene. St George is pictured in armour, bearing a cross, with sword drawn. According to Sylvia P Beamon, author of *Exploring Royston Cave, a Simplified Guide*, the importance of this particular saint was that he 'rescues the lady (that is the church) from the devil or oppressor, represented by the dragon'. St George's sword points towards thirteen figures, thought to be Jesus and his twelve disciples.

As well as the apparitions at Antioch, Jerusalem and Acre,

the Knights Templar apparently believed St George appeared at the 1177 St Catherine's Day victory in Ramleh, riding alongside the leper ruler of Jerusalem, Baldwin IV.

THE BATTLE OF AGINCOURT

'CRY GOD FOR HARRY! England and St George!' These words, penned by William Shakespeare in his play *Henry V*, sum up the extent to which the martyr had become linked to the English military by the fifteenth century. On Henry's departure for Normandy in 1415, the people of England were asked to down tools and head to church to pray to the saint for the safe return of their monarch. During the French campaign, Henry also declared that his troops, and his troops alone, must wear the cross of St George in battle.

His first move was to conquer the town of Harfleur, demanding that the flag of St George be flown over it. In early October he set out for Calais, an English stronghold, so that his troops could recuperate and rearm themselves over the winter. After an eighteen-day march across rough terrain, with many soldiers suffering from dysentery and exhaustion, they found their way barred by a much larger French army. Exact figures are still not known, but many historians believe that of the 9,000 or so English soldiers who left Harfleur, just under 6,000 made it as far as Agincourt. The French force is thought to have been around three times larger.

On 24 October 1415 the two armies camped facing each other over open ground, and on the morning of the 25th Henry V deployed his army. With the clever use of long-bowmen and stakes in the ground to divert the French cavalry, the lesser army prevailed. Again, many claimed that the spectre of St George appeared on the battlefield and spurred the terrified soldiers on to victory.

Henry's triumphant return to London was marked with an elaborate pageant which included a giant figure holding an axe and the keys to the city, as well as a large statue of St George which stood inside a specially constructed tower. Some sources claim that a vision of the saint once again appeared to welcome the king back to his English home.

An anonymous fifteenth-century poem, which entreats us to 'love St George, Our Lady knight,' speaks of his appearance at Agincourt in the same verse as his slaying of the dragon.

> He keped the mad from dragon's dread,
> And fraid all France and put to flight.
> At Agincourt – the crownecle ye red –
> The French him se formest in fight

Which translates as:

He kept the maid from the dragon's dread
And frightened all France, and put to flight.
At Agincourt – in the chronicle you read –
The French saw him foremost in the fight.

THE WARS OF THE ROSES

AS THE SON of Agincourt victor Henry V, the child king Henry VI was closely associated with St George, who was invoked many times at his coronation. Ironically, his enemy and eventual deposer Edward IV also revered the martyr saint and, in an effort to gain the support of the English people, let it be known that he constantly prayed to him. He defeated Henry in 1461 and ruled until the original monarch was reinstated, for just six months, in 1470–71. After he reclaimed the crown Edward IV began to rebuild St George's Chapel at Windsor, at vast cost, in gratitude for the saint's help in his victory.

WORLD WAR I

THE SUPERSTITIOUS soldiers of the medieval era were not the only ones to report sighting St George at crucial moments in military campaigns. A few of those fighting in the First World War claimed to have been helped by visions as well.

In October 1915 the *New York Times* reported the publication of a pamphlet by Ralph Shirley, editor of the *Occult Review*, entitled 'The Angel Warriors at Le Mons'. In it, Mr Shirley cited several apparitions of St George reported from the fields of Flanders in August 1914.

One such story was told by a Miss Phyllis Campbell, who had been a nurse in hospital in France for several months when she was asked to attend an injured fusilier who was asking for a holy picture. 'The idea of an English soldier making such a request at such a time seemed curious but she hurried off to attend to his needs,' says the article, which then quotes the surprised nurse:

'He was propped in a corner, his left arm tied up in a peasant woman's headkerchief, and his head newly bandaged. He should have been in a state of collapse from loss of blood, for his uniform was in tatters and soaked and caked with blood, and his face paper-white under the dirt of conflict. He looked at me with courageous eyes and asked for a picture, or a medal (he did not care which) of St George.

'I asked if he was a Catholic. No, he was a Wesleyan minister and he wanted a picture or medal of St George because he had seen him on a white horse, leading the British at Vitry-le-François when the Allies had turned.

'There was a Royal Field Artillery man, wounded in the leg, sitting beside him on the floor. He saw my look of amazement and hastened in. "It's true, sister," he said. "We all saw it.

'"First there was this sort of yellow mist, sort of risin' on the Germans as they come on to the top of a hill – come on like a solid wall, they did – springing out of the earth, just solid, no end to 'em. I just give up. No more fighting the whole German race, thinks I; it's all up with us. Next up comes this funny cloud of light and when it clears off there's a tall man with yellow hair, in golden armour, on a white horse, holding his sword up and his mouth open, as if he was saying, 'Come on, boys. I'll put the kybosh on the devils!' And before you could say 'knife' the Germans had turned and we were after 'em, fighting like ninety. We had a few scores to settle, sister, and we fair settled 'em."

'Both these soldiers "knew it was St George," because "had they not seen him with his sword on every quid they'd ever had".'

The French soldiers fighting alongside the British swore the vision was of St Michael, also seen as a patron saint of warriors and a dragon slayer, who they believed helped them secure many victories in the Hundred Years' War. Miss Campbell described the French wounded as being in 'a curiously exalted condition – a sort of rapture of happiness'.

In a separate report, sent to the Higher Thought Centre in South Kensington, an officer claimed to have seen a vision of St George during fierce fighting at Mons, also in August 1914.

He plainly saw an apparition representing St George, the exact counterpart of a picture that hangs today in a London restaurant. So terrible was their plight at the time that the officer could not refrain from appealing to the vision to help them. Then, as if the enemy had also seen the apparition, the Germans abandoned their positions in precipitate terror. In other instances, men have reported seeing clouds of celestial horsemen hovering over British lines.

In conclusion, Mr Shirley doubted whether the visions had actually appeared and admitted that they were 'clothed upon by the imagination of the beholder to an almost limitless extent'.

The *New York Times* reported that clergy were uncomfortable with these reports from the front line, viewing them as 'dangerous, threatening a return to medieval superstition'.

THE GEORGE CROSS

IN 1940, as war raged in Europe and Britain suffered the Blitz, King George VI wanted a way to reward the courage and fortitude of ordinary Brits – a civilian equivalent to the military Victoria Cross. The George Cross was introduced to honour 'acts of great heroism or of the most conspicuous courage in circumstances of extreme danger'. The silver cross, designed by Percy Metcalfe, bore the image of St George slaying the dragon and the words 'For Gallantry' around the outside, as well as the king's monogram GVI. The George Medal, for lesser acts of bravery, also bears a picture of the saint and the mythical beast.

The George Cross was awarded to the island of Malta after it repelled repeated attacks from Italy and Germany during the siege of 1941–42. With the inhabitants near starvation from lack of supplies the king sent a letter in April 1942 in which he told the island's governor, 'To honour her brave people I award the George Cross to the Island Fortress of Malta to bear witness to a heroism and devotion that will long be famous in history.'

Incidentally, the Russians beat King George VI to it with the

Cross of St George, awarded for extreme bravery since 1807, and the St George Medal, awarded for lesser acts of bravery since 1878.

CHAPTER FIVE

England's Own

> In left-wing circles it is always felt that there is
> something slightly disgraceful in being an Englishman,
> and that it is a duty to snigger at every English
> institution, from horse racing to suet puddings. It is a
> strange fact, but it is unquestionably true, that almost
> any English intellectual would feel more ashamed of
> standing to attention during 'God Save the King' than
> stealing from a poor box.
>
> GEORGE ORWELL

D ESPITE HIS STATUS as the patron saint of England,
there is little evidence that St George ever set foot
on British soil. However, stories which sprung up
in the medieval age, when the cult of the saint was becoming
popular, give him some presence in the country, varying from a
brief visit as an envoy to Diocletian through to a later retelling
which portrayed him as a native of Coventry and raising three
children there.

In fact the first written mention of George was in the late

seventh century and came ironically from Scotland, from the pen of an Irishman. Adamnan, who also chronicled the life of St Columba, was abbot on the island of Iona from 679 to 704 and passed on extraordinary stories told to him by a travelling bishop called Arculf. One such tale involved a man who promised a horse to St George in return for safe passage from Diospolis. When his journey was over the traveller reneged on his deal but St George made the horse unbiddable until the man fulfilled his end of the bargain. This story, along with the legend of the martyrdom of St George, was repeated by the English historian known as the Venerable Bede (673–735). He identified the saint's persecutor as a Persian king called Dacian, the name repeated by Voragine in the *Golden Legend*.

In the year 1000 Ælfric, archbishop of York, published the *Passion of St George*, which again told the story of the martyrdom but interestingly gave the saint no military background, instead referring to him as a 'rich earldorman' or nobleman. The dragon legend was still not mentioned, which begs the question as to whether George's image as a knight on horseback and his connection with chivalry came entirely from fanciful medieval romanticism rather than fact. However, even the earliest depictions of the saint portray him as a soldier, so, whether it was fact or fiction, the knight story clearly struck a chord.

Although the Normans brought their devotion to St George to English shores in 1066, there is some evidence that his popularity was growing before they arrived. The church at

Fordington in Dorset, which was mentioned in King Alfred's will, was the first to be named in his honour and the Viking king Canute (*c.*995–1035) built a monastery to him at Thetford in Norfolk. The tympanum above the door of the Fordington church also boasts one of the earliest images of the saint, *c.*1100. Interestingly, news of the ghostly apparitions on the battlefields of Jerusalem and Antioch would have reached England shortly before this was produced, and the saint is shown fighting an army of soldiers, some of whom are kneeling in submission and one of whom is being speared in the mouth. A set of paintings, known as the Lewes group, was produced on the walls of Sussex churches at around the same time and also shows the saint in battle.

With the returning crusaders full of stories of how the spirit of St George had protected them in conflict, the cult grew significantly in the twelfth and thirteenth centuries, and in 1222 a meeting of Church elders known as the Council of Oxford, led by Archbishop of Canterbury Stephen Langton, declared 23 April St George's Day. They stopped short of naming him patron saint of England, however, and some historians believe that they merely named him as a secondary saint, to be revered but not celebrated as a feast day.

UK TOUR

THE GROWING LOVE for the saint in the Middle Ages led to tales of a visit to England on the orders of the Roman emperor Diocletian. While here, George was said to have become close to Empress Helena, wife of the Roman ruler of Britain Constantius and mother of the future Christian emperor Constantine I. It was she, legend has it, who discovered in Palestine the cross on which Jesus had been crucified. This was uncovered with two others, thought to be those of the thieves Dismas and Gestus, who were executed alongside Christ. Helena found a local woman suffering from a terminal illness and asked her to touch all three crosses. The first two had no effect but the third cured the woman and was declared the True Cross. Helena built the church of the Holy Sepulchre on the site of the discovery and, because of her friendship with the by-this-time-martyred George, ordered a church dedicated to him to be built next door.

Other legends have him as a soldier serving in York with the young Constantine, who would go on to reverse the persecution of Christians in the Roman Empire. While in the country, St George was also said to have gone to Glastonbury to visit the tomb of Joseph of Arimathea, and to have travelled to the Welsh stronghold of Christianity at Caerleon-on-Usk.

OUSTING ST EDMUND

THE FIRST REFERENCE to George as patron saint of England was in 1351. Up until that date the martyred king St Edmund had been recognised as England's protector. Born on Christmas Day in 841, the Christian king ruled over East Anglia from 856. In 869, when a large Viking force arrived on his shores, Edmund led his army against them in an attempt to defend England. Defeated, he was captured and ordered to renounce his faith and become a puppet king for the heathen invaders. Edmund refused, telling them, 'Living or dead, nothing shall separate me from the love of Christ.' As a result he was tortured, some say with hot irons and some by being shot through with arrows, before being beheaded at Hoxne, in Sussex, on 20 November 869. Some thirty-three years later his body was taken from its grave at the small church in Hoxne to the town of Bedricsworth in Suffolk. There he was finally laid to rest and a shrine was built in his honour. The town's name changed to Edmundston and eventually it became Bury St Edmunds, the borough of St Edmund, not, as popular legend has it, a reference to the fact that he is buried there.

Another candidate for the role of English patron saint was Edward the Confessor, although he was less relevant to the general population, being the patron saint of kings. The son of Ethelred the Unready, he was one of the last Anglo-Saxon kings and reigned 1042–66. Famed for piety and kindness, he founded Westminster Abbey, where his remains were laid to rest two years after his 1161 canonisation. His chronicler Osbert de Clare recorded several miracles that the king had performed, including healing by touch, and Osbert travelled to Rome to help secure the sainthood from Pope Gregory III.

These two saints seemed to have existed as parallel patrons of England until the increased popularity of St George finally usurped them. Richard the Lionheart, despite his connections with George, was also known for a devotion to St Edmund. Richard's great-nephew Edward I (reigned 1272–1307) intro-duced the practice of displaying St George's flag alongside the other two's for his Welsh campaign in 1277.

Even after the 1351 declaration in an official document that 'the English nation call upon St George as being their special patron, particularly in war', the three were often invoked together. A 1360 stained-glass image in Heydour, Lincolnshire, for example, shows all three saints in armour, a reference to their roles as joint protectors of England. At his coronation in 1377 Richard II wore St Edmund's slippers and Edward the Confessor's coat and the latter's crown was placed on his head.

The reference to war in the declaration suggests this new adoration of St George was directly linked to the crusades and the invocation of the saint by Richard the Lionheart in 1199. The fact that this statement came in the reign of Edward III is no surprise. Not only was he one of the most militarily successful English kings of the Middle Ages, he was also a huge champion of St George. After the rebuilding of the chapel at Windsor Castle, the king had it rededicated to bear the name of the soldier saint rather than Edward the Confessor, for whom it had been previously named. This was a clear indication of his reverence and served to forge a strong link between St George and the monarchy.

THE SAINT OF KINGS

EDWARD III

A BOY KING, Edward succeeded to the throne at the age of fourteen, in 1327, following a plot to depose his father, Edward II, by his mother and her lover. His interest in St George was evident from the beginning, as a document called the Milemete Treatise, still in existence, shows. The manuscript was a gift from the king's clerk Master Walter of Milemete, at the very start of his reign, and is decorated with an image of Edward being presented with his arms by St George himself. Both are in armour, associating the saint once more with knighthood, and George has a sheathed sword while the young king holds a spear. The document was a sort of monarch's manual, spelling out the responsibilities and moral values that a king must take on, and the image serves to emphasise the necessity for chivalry and urges the king to emulate his saintly hero.

Paintings from later in Edward's reign, which hung on the east wall of St Stephen's chapel in the palace of Westminster but have since been destroyed, showed St George with the king, his wife Queen Phillippa and their ten children. The king was also known to have owned a vial supposedly of the saint's blood, mentioned in a list of royal relics. During his many military campaigns it is known that small statuettes of St George were given to those fighting alongside Edward. According to the historian Thomas of Walsingham, Edward prayed to his patron at the siege of Calais, in 1347, before drawing his sword and crying, 'Ha! St Edward! Ha! St George!' He then led his troops into renewed battle. The subsequent English victory strengthened his allegiance to his patron.

THE ORDER OF THE GARTER

In 1344 there was some suggestion at court that King Arthur's legendary round table be somehow resurrected for present-day knights of the realm. Instead, Edward III decided to found his own chivalric order, the Order of the Garter, which he put under St George's patronage. Founded in 1348, the order consisted of two groups of twelve knights, led by the king and his eldest son Edward, known as the Black Prince. Membership was a prestigious honour bestowed as a reward for loyalty to the crown and outstanding military achievement, and those joining were expected to abide by the values of chivalry and show unswerving loyalty to the king. The two groups, seated beside the high altar on opposite sides of the chapel in Windsor, facing one other, could also compete against each other in the chivalric contests of the day. As well as a chance to indulge in pomp and ceremony, the order was a useful way for Edward to keep the powerful nobles of England on his side.

The name of the new group, legend has it, originated from an incident involving Joan, countess of Salisbury, who was rumoured to be Edward's lover. At a state function the renowned beauty was said to have lost a garter which the gallant king retrieved and tied around his own leg. This caused many of the guests to snigger but the king reacted with the comment 'Honi soit qui mal y pense' (Shame on he who thinks evil of it). The theory is that his elevation of the garter to a status symbol was a rebuke to those whose laughter he found less than chivalrous. Although the story provides a pleasingly romantic origin for the name, it is more likely that the garter was a reference to the leather straps with which knights secured their armour. The knights of the order, which survives today, wear a blue garter just below the left knee and a 'George', a badge depicting the saint on horseback slaying the dragon.

After rededicating the Windsor chapel, Edward filled it with images of St George, including wooden carvings of his life and martyrdom and a statue of George and the dragon. One particular piece, an alabaster tableau which was commissioned to go behind the high altar, was transported from Nottingham on ten carts, each pulled by ten horses. The framework of the piece contained jewelled reliquaries holding religious relics including a section of the True Cross obtained by Edward I. The chapel also housed reliquaries containing some of the saint's bones.

A feast to mark the inception of the new order was held at Windsor on 23 April 1349. Contemporary historian Geoffrey le Baker, in his *Chronicon Angliae temporibus Edwardi II et Edwardi III*, described the knights' attire. 'They were all clothed like the king in cloaks of russet powered with garters, dark blue in colour, and also had similar garters on their right legs with blue mantles bearing shields of the arms of St George,' he wrote. 'They sat at the table together, in honour of the Holy Martyr from whom they took the title of this most noble brotherhood, calling the company of these men of "St George de la Gartiere".'

Surprisingly, considering the emphasis on male chivalry, the order was open to women, under the title Dame de la Confraternité de St George, until 1509, when a new ruling meant that only a reigning queen could join. In 1987 women were once more afforded full membership rights, and the current order, headed by Queen Elizabeth II and the Prince of Wales, includes Baroness Thatcher and Baroness Soames. There is also room for foreign dignitaries, with the current crop of 'Stranger Knights and Ladies' comprising Grand Duke Jean of Luxembourg, Queen Margrethe II of Denmark, King Carl XVI Gustaf of Sweden, King Juan Carlos of Spain, Queen Beatrix of the Netherlands, King Harald V of Norway and the Emperor Akihito of Japan.

HENRY V

After the apparition at the Battle of Agincourt and subsequent victory, St George's status in England and in the court grew once more. In 1415, the year of Agincourt, archbishop Chichele declared St George's Day a 'greater double' feast day and ordered it to be observed like Christmas and Easter, a holiday from normal work when everyone attended church. The saint was to be considered 'the special patron and protector of the English nation'.

In 1416 a special banquet was held at Windsor Castle in honour of the Hungarian king Sigismund, who was to be inducted into the Order of the Garter. The honoured guest brought with him a priceless gift, the saint's heart, which was placed alongside the other relics in St George's chapel. The impressive spread provided for the two kings included various 'sotylties', thought to be cakes or pastry confections in the shape of St George, one with an angel fixing his armour, another with George slaying a dragon and a third with the saint and the rescued princess leading the dragon towards the town.

Henry's death in 1422 was marked by a famous image in the Bedford Hours, a manuscript created a year later to mark the marriage of the new regent, Henry's brother the duke of Bedford, to Anne of Burgundy. The duke is seen kneeling before St George, who is wearing the full regalia of the Order of the Garter, and many historians argue that the scene shows Henry, in the guise of his patron, handing over the regency of France until his son and successor, just nine months when he died, is old enough to take over.

HENRY VI

The infant king grew up steeped in his father's devotion to St George and carried on the traditions associated with him. In November 1429 the seven year old was crowned at St Peter's church in Westminster and once again a sumptuous feast kept the artistic pastry chefs busy. Fabyan's Chronicle, published posthumously in 1516, described the scene (although it was slightly out on the monarch's age).

> Kynge Henry beynge upon the age of six yeres was solempnly crowned in Seynt Peters church of Westmynster . . . and after that solempnzacion the sayd church fynysshed, an honourable feest in the great halle of Westmynster was kepte . . . Between the third course was a sotyltie of our Lady syttynge with her childe in her lappe and she holdyng a crowne in her hande. Seynt George and Seynt Denys knelynge on eyther syde presentyd to her kyng Henryes fygure berynge in hande this balade as foloweth:
>> O blessyd Lady, Cristys moder dere
>> And thou seynt George that called art her Knyght.

During the ceremony the king's champion Sir Philip Dimmock rode into the hall dressed in the armour of St George to declare the boy the rightful ruler of England.

A year later, when he set off for France to be crowned king there, an anonymous poem called on the saint to protect him on his journey.

> Seynt George, our ladyes knight,
> On whom alle Englond hath byleve,
> Shew us thy helpe to God almyght,
> And kepe oure kyng from all myscheve.

In 1440 Henry founded Eton College as a charitable institution to provide education for seventy poor boys and give them the chance to move on to King's College, Cambridge. He gave the school a number of religious relics, including part of the True Cross and Christ's crown of thorns, and many images of St George decorated the magnificent buildings. The buttresses of the antechapel boast a huge figure of the saint slaying the dragon, which is paired with a similarly large statue of St Edmund.

As previously mentioned (*see page 44*), Henry's nemesis Edward IV, who deposed the king twice during the Wars of the Roses, was also a firm devotee of St George and rebuilt the chapel in his name at Windsor at vast cost in gratitude for the saint's assistance in regaining the throne. The fact that both sides claimed George as their patron shows how established the saint's cult in England had become, and how strongly he symbolised England and the monarchy in noble minds.

HENRY VII

The instability brought about by the Wars of the Roses ended with the accession of Henry VII in 1485, and despite his Welsh roots, his reign saw interest in the saint peak. For his coronation a St George's cross was made from six yards of red velvet, and shortly before his death in 1509 he commissioned an altarpiece from a Flemish artist known as Maynard, which depicted the king, Queen Elizabeth and their seven children with St Michael and St George. Elizabeth and four of her children were dead by the time the painting was commissioned, and the scene shows the archangel Michael standing between the males and females of the family, who kneel in prayer. Behind them an oversized George and dragon fight to the death, watched by the legendary princess and her lamb.

Henry VII was known to put great store by St George's day and Fabyan's Chronicle again describes one particular 23 April, when he received a priceless relic as a gift from King Louis of France. 'Upon Saynt Georges day the Kyng went in procession in Poules church where was shewn a legge of Saynt George closed in sylver whych was newly sent to the kyng.' This same relic was mentioned in his will, in which Henry specified that the leg and a section of the True Cross should be brought out and placed on the high altar at Windsor for special feast days.

> Also we give and bequeathe . . . the preciouse relique of oon
> of the leggs of St George set in silver parcell gilte, which
> came to the hands of our broder and cousyn Loys of
> Fraunce the tyme that he wan and recover'd the citie of
> Millein, and was geven and sent to us by our cousyne the
> cardinal of Amboys legate of Fraunce : the which pece of the
> holie Crosse and leg of Saincte George we wol bee set upon
> the said aulter for the garnishing of the same upon all
> principal and solempne fests.

Another bequest was a solid gold statue for the same altar. Even in death the king and his wife were guarded by their patron saint, who appears twice on their tomb in Westminster Abbey.

HENRY VIII

Although he is chiefly remembered for his wives and the split from the Catholic church, Henry was also the monarch that finally established St George as the single patron saint of England in the hearts and minds of the nation. As well as adopting the red cross as the country's flag during his reign (1509–47), he issued coins that bore the image of the saint engaged in battle with the dragon. The breastplate of his own suit of armour featured a large engraving of George and the dragon while the backplate had an image of St Barbara, the fourth-century martyr who was locked in a tower by her pagan father and beheaded by him when she revealed her conversion to Christianity. His horse irons also told the martyrdom tales of the two saints.

After his break with Rome, brought about by the Pope's refusal to grant an annulment of his marriage to Catherine of Aragon, the king banned most Catholic feasts but St George's Day was among the few celebrations spared. Fabyan's Chronicle records that on 22 July 1541 'there was a proclamation that no holy daye should be kept except our Ladyes dayes, the apostle

Evangelists, St George's and St Mary Magdalen'. St George, in the king's eyes, symbolised the strength of the nation as it stood in religious isolation.

However, Henry's son Edward VI was soon to undo much of the country's devotion to the saint and send George's popularity plummeting.

THE GUILDS

THE MIDDLE AGES also saw the rise of powerful guilds of St George. These groups were open only to men and women of the social elite, and offered further prestige, setting them apart from the other guilds, which catered mainly for tradesmen. These organisations sprung up in towns and cities across England including Norwich, Coventry, Reading, Leicester, York, Hull and Salisbury. Chichester founded a guild of St George in 1386, and a revealing insight into its power provided is offered by a local law which stated that only members of the guild could vote for the city's member of parliament.

The guilds were not merely tools for wielding power. The groups met for mass, often in their own chapel, collected alms, even provided pensions for their members and were committed to celebrating the saint's feast day together. The celebrations were elaborate affairs which involved marches through the streets known as the Riding of the George. The procession was made up of people in various costumes and always included the saint, a princess and a dragon.

One of the most important guilds was that of Leicester, set up relatively late, at the beginning of the fifteenth century. Its services were held in the chapel of St George within St Martin's church, where a raised platform displayed a life-sized figure of the saint on horseback. In her 1908 book *St George for Merrie England* Margaret H Bulley wrote,

> Once a year this figure was drawn round the town in the great procession called 'The Ryding of the George', in which the Mayor and Corporation and all the townsfolk were obliged to take part. At one time, however, this custom must have fallen into abeyance, for in an old deed of 1523 we read, 'Whosoeur be the maister of Seynt Georgis Gylde shall cause the George to be rydyn according to the olde auncient costome y at ys to sey betwyx Sent Georgys day and Wytsondey.'

Another huge spectacle was the Riding in Norwich, where one of the most powerful guilds was established in 1385 and granted a royal charter by Henry V in 1417. The ancient charter of the city reveals the guild's rule,

It is ordeined be the comon ascent of the Fraternite that all
the Brethern and Susteren of the Fraternite shullen halwen
the day of Seynt George yerely on what day so it befalle.

Also ther kepe her dyvine servise of both even-songes and
messe in the cathedral forseide & other observaunces of the
Fraternite ordeyned ... be assent of the bretheren yer schul
ordeyne and pflx [fix] a day on which day alle bretheren &
susteren schull kepen all her observaunces of her Divine
Service aforn reherced & kepe her Riding & haven and kepen
& weren her Clothing & holden her Fest.

The Norwich Guild chose actors to take the roles of
St George, the princess, the king, the dragon, henchmen and
torch carriers. After a breakfast of bread, cheese and wine the
procession began at the cathedral, headed by the carrier of an
ancient sword with a dragon's head engraved on it, behind
whom rode the 'George' in silver armour and a fur-trimmed
gown. Then came the henchmen and the 'Lady', who was also
on horseback. The dragon, which was constructed from iron
hoops and wood and, according to civic records frequently
repaired, could spit fire and smoke through the use of gun-
powder. Its mouth could open and shut through a system of
levers operated by the actor, earning the beast the nickname of
Snap, and as well as sparring with the mounted saint throughout the procession, he would frequently charge at spectators,
delighting and no doubt terrifying the small children in the

crowd. After the players arrived at a wood near the city, the battle between George and the dragon was re-enacted before everybody returned to the cathedral for a service, followed by a huge feast hosted by the guild.

The Norwich festivities were typical of celebrations which took place all over the country, helping to establish St George's Day as an important event in the English calendar.

PEOPLE'S PATRON

T HE GUILD PROCESSIONS, which were attended by a large proportion of the local population, were just one way in which the people of England showed their devotion to the saint during the Middle Ages. St George was a leading figure in plays and comical sketches known as drolls put on by players throughout the country. Miracle plays, performed by travelling groups on elaborately decorated portable stages, often focused on the dragon legend and were the forerunners of mummers' plays, which became popular in the early nineteenth century.

In country houses richer families would be amused by dramatisations performed by their children or even by the servants. In the Paston Letters, a collection of papers written between 1422 and 1509 by the wealthy Paston family, one writer bemoans the loss of a manservant who seems to have been kept in employment because of his ability to act rather than serve. 'I have kept him thys iii yere to pleye Seynt Jage and Robin Hood and the Sheryff of Notyngham,' the letter reads.

St George also appears in many traditional songs such as the Padstow May Day Song, which includes the lyric, 'Oh where is St George, oh where is he-o / He's out in the longboat, all on the salt sea-o.'

CHAPTER SIX

The Green Man

WHILE THE LEGEND of St George is firmly rooted in Christianity and martyrdom, he also has some links with the pagan figure known as the Green Man. This symbol of fertility, often seen dressed in leaves, represents the rebirth of spring after the death of winter. The fact that this pre-Christian icon is often called Green George, and that the date of St George's Day coincides with the beginning of spring, has led to the two becoming inextricably linked.

In the *Golden Legend* Jacobus de Voragine points out that the saint's very name has an agricultural origin.

> George is said of geos, which is as much to say as earth, and orge that is tilling. So George is to say as tilling the earth, that is his flesh. And S. Austin saith, in libro de Trinitate that, good earth is in the height of the mountains, in the temperance of the valleys, and in the plain of the fields. The first is good for herbs being green, the second to vines, and

the third to wheat and corn. Thus the blessed George was
high in despising low things, and therefore he had verdure in
himself, he was attemperate by discretion, and therefore he
had wine of gladness, and within he was plane of humility,
and thereby put he forth wheat of good works.

The deaths and resurrections of the martyr during his
ordeal strengthen his links to fertility and rebirth and throughout the world he is invoked as the spring saint. One account of
his life, from the aforementioned Pasicrates manuscript (*see page
16*), known as the Vienna Palimpsest, has him performing a
miracle on wooden benches, making them grow roots and bear
fruit.

Throughout the world St George has become associated
with the reawakening of nature. One Russian proverb warns,
'There is no spring without George,' and Estonians say, 'With
his key George makes the grass grow.' In Lithuania he seen
as the keeper of the keys of summer. In many countries
St George's Day is marked with green plants being placed
near homes, and in Greece, where he is the patron saint of
shepherds, his day is one of the most important feasts in the
Orthodox Church. In France statues of St George used to be
carried through the cherry orchards to encourage a good crop,
and in the Ukraine his day is marked with a blessing over the
crops.

'Perhaps the richness of the tradition accumulated on St

George's Day should rather be viewed in the light of the fact that the Greek form Georgius means a ploughman, a cultivator of land,' wrote Estonian folklorist Mall Hiiemäe. 'And when trying to divine the ancient predecessor of the holiday, one should better consider such tradition that is connected with spring-time vegetation as well as the concentration of special customs on certain pre-Christian dates to mark the awakening of nature and the arrival of spring.'

AL-KHIDR

THROUGH THE STORY of the Green Man, George also has close ties with the Islamic icon al-Khidr, also known as the Green One, who is said to have found the well of life from which immortality can be gained and drank the waters, leaving him able to resurrect himself after death. Other stories say he bathed in it three times and turned green as a result, leaving verdant footprints wherever he trod thereafter. As well as the ability to rejuvenate, also attributed to George, the water theme is a clear parallel, as the dragon legend includes the founding of a church housing a fountain of restorative water.

THE HEALING SAINT

THE NAME of St George is often invoked to ward off or conquer disease. In Normandy he has a healing spring named after him, and in Germany he is one of the 'fourteen holy helpers' revered for their ability to cure the sick. In 530 a deacon known as Theodosius claimed that the saint's remains rested at a tomb in Lydda, and recorded miracles that had occurred there, with the sick being healed on the site.

The saint's ability to heal himself during his persecution, with the help of God, may be the origin of his connection to the conquering of diseases, and he is often linked to disfiguring illnesses such as leprosy, the plague and syphilis, possibly due to his victory over the foul-smelling and scaly dragon. The Pasicrates manuscript tells of him healing the sick and even has him raising the dead.

In the *Golden Legend* the church built in his honour and that of the Virgin Mary leads to the miraculous sprouting of a fountain. 'The king built a magnificent church there in honour of Blessed Mary and St George, and from the altar flowed a spring whose waters cure all diseases.'[5] It is also mentioned that

5. William Granger Ryan translation.

the saint's remains, said to lie in a chapel between Jerusalem and Jaffa, can cure madness. 'In his tomb is a hole that a man may put in his hand. And when a Saracen, being mad, is brought thither, and if he put his head in the hole he shall anon be made perfectly whole, and have his wit again.'

Writing in 1866, Elizabeth Finn observed,

> The Arabs believe that St George can restore mad people to their senses; and to say a person has been sent to St George's, is equivalent to saying he has been sent to a madhouse.
>
> It is singular that the Moslem Arabs share this veneration for St George, and send their mad people to be cured by him, as well as the Christians. But they commonly call him El Khudder – The Green – according to their favorite manner of using epithets instead of names. Why he should be called green, however, I cannot tell – unless it is from the colour of his horse. Gray horses are called green in Arabic.

A Christian monastery was established in Pomorie, Bulgaria, in the seventh century. During the Ottoman invasion in the fourteenth century the building was sadly destroyed and some 400 years later a Turkish administrator named Selim Bey established a farm on the site. Dying from an incurable disease, Selim dreamt that he had found healing waters on his land and the following day searched for the spot he had seen in his dream. In his yard he came across a marble bas-relief of St George beneath which flowed a spring. After drinking the water, he was cured of his illness and his whole family converted to Christianity, building a chapel on the site and laying the foundations of the present-day monastery.

When his wife died, Selim became the father superior and donated his land and wealth to the monastery. The bas-relief of the legend can still be seen in the monastery.

CHAPTER SEVEN

The Fall of a Hero

THE REFORMATION in the sixteenth century spelled the beginning of the end for devotees of our patron saint. With the Catholic Church ridiculed by Lutherans and Calvinists, the cult of saints began to be seen as idolatrous and Protestant reformers saw St George as part of the old Roman establishment. John Calvin called George a larva, meaning a scarecrow, and another Protestant work denounced him as 'a deity created by some madde and idle brains for the poor people to fall down and worship'.[6]

With the accession of Edward VI in 1547, the saint's connection with the Anglican Church immediately began to slip. That same year parliament passed a law banning the processions of the guilds, many of which were a St George's Day tradition. The guilds themselves lost many of their powers, and although some reorganised or renamed themselves, the parades were largely over. A warden at St Martin's church in Leicester, where

6. Unattributed source quoted in Helen Gibson, 'St George the Ubiquitous', *Saudi Aramco World*, November/December 1971.

the procession had been a huge event, recorded the sale of a valuable asset in his 1547 records: 'Sold to Henry Mayblay, the horse that the George rode on, 12d.'

The revision of the prayer book in 1548 saw the gospel and epistle for St George's day scrapped and in 1552 the bishop of London banned the marking of the day altogether. The *Grey Friars Chronicle* recorded, 'Item also where it hathe bene of ane olde custome that sent George shude be kepte holy day thorrow alle England, the byshoppe of London commandyd that it shudde not be kepte, and no more it was not.'

The Norwich guild, who had so revelled in the feast day, changed their name to the Company and Citizens of St George and decided they had no choice but to celebrate without their beloved martyr and his lady, sometimes called Margaret after the other dragon-slaying saint. But Snap survived. In 1558 it was announced 'that there be neyther George nor Margett, but for pastime the Dragon to come and shew himself as in other years'. He lasted in town celebrations until 1731 and is now preserved in the town's museum. A brief respite for St George's Day pageantry came under Catholic Queen Mary but the accession of her sister Elizabeth meant a new hatred of all things considered close to Catholicism and a rise in Puritanism. Images of St George were once more banned from guild processions, although again the dragon was permitted.

In his *History of the World*, published in 1614, Elizabethan adventurer and courtier Sir Walter Raleigh voiced dismay that the English people had chosen St George as their champion and went as far as to dismiss him as an imaginary person. After mentioning the old castle of St George five miles from the ancient Syrian city of Ptolomais, he wrote,

> And though for the credit of St George killing the Dragon I leave every man to his own belief, yet I cannot but think that, if the Kings of England had not some probable record of that his memorable act among many others; it was strange that the order full of honour which Edward III founded, and which his successors royally have continued should have borne his name, seeing the world had not that scarcity of saints in those days as the English were driven to make such an erection upon a fable or person feigned.

He goes on to quote Dutch clergyman and writer Adrichomius' version of the legend. 'In this place which by the inhabitants is called Cappadocia, not far from Berytus, men say that the famous knight of Christ, St George, did rescue the king's daughter from a huge dragon, and, having killed the beast, delivered the virgin to her parent. In memory of which deed a church was after built there.' Raleigh then asserts that this story is merely allegorical and insists it is better to believe George never existed than to revere the other, less savoury George of Cappadocia (*see page 14*). 'If this authority suffice not, we may rather make the story allegorical, figuring the victory of Christ, than accept of George the Arian bishop mentioned by Marcellinus.' However, while the court and the Church were distancing themselves from the country's adopted saint, the people's adoration was strengthened by Richard Johnson's retelling of the legend, published in 1576.

THE COVENTRY CONNECTION

The Most Famous History of the Seven Champions of Christendom by Richard Johnson claimed, rather bizarrely, that the saint was the son of Lord Albert, the high steward of Coventry, and the grandson of the king. Born with three birthmarks, in the shapes of a dragon, a cross and a garter, the infant is kidnapped by an evil sorceress who spares his life and raises him as her own. As he approaches manhood, however, he vows to leave her to seek adventure.

She begs him to remain, showing him the six champions of Christendom whom she has kept under a spell, and promising he will be the greatest of them if he stays. He refuses. She then offers him the swiftest of seven powerful horses, but still he says he must leave. She offers a magical suit of invincible armour but once again he refuses to stay. Finally, in desperation, she gives him her magic wand, the source of her powers, which he accepts before using it to open a great cleft in the rock, where he traps her for eternity.

Free from the enchantress, he frees the other six champions, themselves all patron saints. They are St Andrew of Scotland, St Patrick of Ireland, St David of Wales, St Denis of France, St James of Spain and St Anthony of Italy. The seven freed saints then take the armour and the seven horses and travel together until such time as they reach a junction of seven paths. There they separate, each choosing a route that leads to a different adventure.

George's path takes him to Egypt where the sultan's daughter Sabra is about to be sacrificed to a ferocious dragon. Her father has promised her hand in marriage to anyone who can save her, which the chilvalrous knight duly does, by plunging a spear into the chest of the beast. Urged on by a rival suitor for Sabra's hand, Almindor, the Black Prince of Morocco, her father seeks to back out of the deal, fearing that his daughter will be converted to Christianity. He sends his potential son-in-law with a message to the king of Persia which, on opening, will mean instant death to the messenger. The king ties St George up in a dungeon full of lions but our hero frees himself and kills them with his bare hands. After stealing a horse, he heads back to Egypt, slaying a deadly giant on the way as well as rescuing St David from an evil wizard by drawing a sword from a stone and thereby breaking the spell that holds him captive.

Seven years after slaying the dragon, he returns to the Egyptian royal palace to find his bride already wed to the evil Almindor, although crucially she is still a virgin 'through the secret virtue of a golden chain steeped in tigers' blood, which she wore seven times double about her ivory neck'. St George reclaims his love and they elope together.

Later they meet the other six champions and together vow to raise armies to conquer the pagan lands which had wronged St George: Egypt, Morocco and Persia. After returning home to England, where he raises troops, George sets off with his soldiers to meet the other armies in Portugal, whence he leads them into battle against Almindor of Morocco. After a fierce speech, the soldiers, 'with a general voice, cried, "To arms, to arms, with victorious George of England!" which noble resolution of the soldiers so rejoiced the English champion, and likewise encouraged the other Christian knights with such a forwardness of mind, that they gave speedy commandment to remove their tents'. They quickly conquer the 'Blackmoor' king and George takes revenge by casting his enemy into a cauldron of boiling oil.

Next the seven champions march for Egypt, to challenge Sabra's father Ptolemy, who immediately surrenders. The seven men decide to show mercy, 'especially St George, who having a heart beautified with a well-spring of pity, not only granted mercy to the whole country, but vouchsafed Ptolemy liberty of life, upon condition that he would perform what he had promised; which was, to forsake his false gods, and believe in our true God, Christ Jesus'.

Back in England, however, his beloved Sabra murders the evil earl of Coventry who threatened to rape her after she refused his advances. On hearing the news St George leaves the armies in Egypt and hurries home, arriving just in time to rescue her from a sentence of death by burning. After the rescue George heads for Persia, this time with his lady at his side. On the way Sabra gives birth to male triplets in an enchanted wood, aided by the fairy queen Porserpine, who bestows on each a gift. After being abducted by a tigress, a lioness and a she-wolf, and rescued by their loving father, the three boys are split up and each sent to a different country to be raised.

> The first, and eldest, whose fortune was to be a soldier, he
> sent to the imperial city of Rome (being then the wonder of
> the world for martial discipline), there by the emperor to be
> trained up. The second, whose fortune was to be a courtly
> prince, he sent to the rich and plentiful country of England,
> being the pride of Christendom for all delightful pleasures:
> the third and last, whose fortune was to be a scholar, he sent
> into Germany, unto the university of Wittenburg, being
> thought at that time to be the excellentest place of learning
> that remained throughout the whole world.

As St George makes his way to Persia, stopping for various adventures and months of feasting on the way, 100,000

Christian troops there enter a five-day battle against a pagan force numbering 300,000. After much spillage of blood on both sides, the vanquished pagans retreat, 'for when they beheld their fields bestrewed with mangled bodies and that the rivers for twenty miles' compass did flow with crimson blood, their hearts began to fail and incontinently fled like sheep before the wolf'. Fortune takes a turn for the worse, however, when the six remaining champions are beguiled by spirits in the form of a hundred beautiful virgins conjured up by a wicked magician.

On arrival, 'St George with his sword made lanes of slaughtered men, and with his angry arm made passage through the thickest of their troops, as though that death had been commander of the battle.' Finding his comrades disrobed and lying in the arms of the enemy's temptresses, he rallies them and breaks the spell, leading them once more to battle and victory.

The saga draws to a close with Sabra meeting her end after falling from her horse into a prickly bush and St George slaying a second dragon, this time in England, and losing his life in the process.

The story, written c.1576, owes more to patriotism than any real connection to Coventry or indeed England. Although the other saints are virtuous and courageous characters, St George is portrayed throughout as the most noble of all. He is frequently called upon to rescue his weaker brothers from the grasp of evil, and in his absence they often falter in their quest.

Beautiful scenes of England are often mentioned and countries further afield are awash with dangerous wild beasts and malevolent magicians. Much is made of St George's invented English lineage while the origins of the others are only mentioned in terms of their patronage.

The message is clear: with St George representing England herself, she is ever ready to step in to help her Christian neighbours against the dark forces of paganism.

The story, and the saint's new English roots, spawned a rash of ballads which added various new twists to the dragon tale, including the ancient romantic device of leaving the damsel in distress tied to a stake while she awaits her fate. A series of chapbooks, or abridged works, based on Johnson's version and published in the eighteenth century, added further fuel to the patriotic claims by stating that the martyr was buried in Windsor.

JOHNSON REBUKED

ANOTHER BOOST to the saint's reputation came when controversial English historian Peter Heylyn looked into his life with the intention of debunking the 'fictions of the Middle Ages'. In *The History of that most famous Saint and Soldier of*

Christ Isus, St George of Cappadocia, published in the 1630s, he promised to 'cleere the history of St George from all further questions'. He dismissed Johnson's account of an English background but concluded that 'the killing of dragons is both feasible and ordinary', including two examples of dragons terrorising the population in villages in Oxfordshire and Surrey to back up his argument.

'Our own chronicles, to go no further, make mention somewhere of a dragon of almost incredible greatnesse found at Hooke-Norton, not faire from Oxen, besides what Hoveden hath reported "de serpentibus in Sussevia visis magna cum admiratione" of serpents seen in Sussex, to the great astonishment of the people,' he wrote.

> Such creatures there are and have beene in being in most
> places; so in Africa especially there where St George is said to
> have killed a dragon ... an African or Lybian dragon, for so is
> reported in the Legend. So why might not George, a soldier
> both of great magnanimity and discretion, God's love and
> goodnesse concurring with him in the act, bee said to kill a
> Dragon, a serpentine creature of great bulke and danger.

The angry writer goes on to chastise 'those Heretickes and atheists' who seek to besmirch the name of St George and states that 'bytwene Jherusalem and porte Japhe by a towne callyd Ramys is a chapell of Saynt George' where the saint's body was buried alongside that of his mother, father and uncle.

As a Scottish king first, Elizabeth's successor James I had even less allegiance to the English saint, and the rise of Puritanism during his son Charles I's reign further damaged the cult of St George. In late 1641 the House of Commons sanctioned the removal and destruction of statues and 'scandalous pictures' of the Trinity, crucifixes and all images of the Virgin Mary. With regular riots in London against the worship of false idols, and the vandalising of churches in the name of Puritanism, statues and images of St George were inevitably consigned to the same fate as those of the Blessed Virgin, with whom he was so associated.

A poem entitled 'Saint George and the Dragon', written during the English Civil War, possibly by General George Monck, Duke of Albermarle, uses the symbol of St George to suggest that the Rump Parliament, which was to try Charles I for treason, was the dragon that England had to slay. A second instalment of the ballad has George defeating the rebel politicians.

> So t'was time for St George,
>
> That Rump to disgorge,
>
> And to send it from whence it first came.[7]

Under the Cromwellian protectorate, from 1649 to 1660, the patron saint of England was sidelined and almost forgotten. The

---

7. Samantha Riches, *St George: Hero, Martyr and Myth.*

lull continued for over a hundred years, although some of the traditional customs, such as the procession and re-enactment of the battle with the dragon, may have been revived in small towns and villages after the restoration of the monarchy.

The fact that two churches dedicated to St George were built in London, in Wapping and Bloomsbury, in the early eighteenth century is evidence that the saint was once again held in high regard by the Church. Travellers to North America took their love of the saint with them, and societies of St George which aimed to help immigrants and provide much-needed food and shelter, sprang up in the New World. According to the Royal Society of St George, the earliest branches were established in New York (1770), Philadelphia (1772) and Charlestown (1773). Further groups were formed in all the large cities, where St George's parades were an annual event, and when the American War of Independence displaced English settlers to Canada, societies were set up there too.

Back in England, however, his cause wasn't helped by the publication, between 1776 and 1788, of *The History of the Decline and Fall of the Roman Empire*, by Edward Gibbon. The historian wrongly identified the saint as the Arian priest and pork sales-man of Cappadocia. In answer to these heinous accusations, in 1792 a London clergyman called the Reverend Milner pub-lished a paper with the snappy title of *A Historical and Critical Inquiry into the existence and character of St George, Patron of England, in which the assertions of Edward Gibbon, Esq. and certain other modern writ-*

ers concerning this Saint are discussed, pointing out the flaws in Gibbon's arguments, but this little-known writer failed to reach the large audience of George's accuser.

As Prince Regent, George IV sought to promote his namesake when he founded the Most Distinguished Order of St Michael and St George in 1818, the purpose of which was to bestow honours for outstanding diplomatic service in Malta and the Ionian Islands, then British possession. In 1879 eligibility was extended to all Commonwealth countries and eventually to women, who would become dames rather than knights. Today the medal depicts George and the dragon on one side and St Michael defeating the devil on the other.

In George IV's reign the British built a church of St George on Corfu and also the Palace of St Michael and St George, which served as the home of the lord high commissioner until 1864. The king also moved the date of his birthday celebrations to 23 April, to mark his allegiance to the saint.

REVIVAL

I N 1875 the famous Liberty department store opened in London in a fabulous mock-Tudor building adorned by a clock with moving figures. A little St George on a white horse can be seen rushing out to slay a dragon with his lance on the hour every hour.

Towards the end of the nineteenth century St George's popularity was growing again. The famous art critic John Ruskin, for example, founded the Guild of St George in 1871 with a dual purpose – to promote patriotism and help the poor. For the first aim St George was an obvious choice but in invoking his name for a charity which sought to address the housing problem in England and provide better conditions for workers he also called upon the English sense of fair play.

Queen Victoria herself became patron of one patriotic movement founded in 1894. According to its website, the Royal Society of St George, which is still going strong today, was set up to promote 'Englishness and the English Way of Life'. In the early twentieth century it attracted many high-profile supporters, including Field Marshal Montgomery, Winston Churchill and Rudyard Kipling. Past presidents include the Duke of

Westminster and Baroness Thatcher, and it has boasted the patronage of every reigning monarch since its inception.

By the turn of the century, many towns were beginning to celebrate the feast day for the first time in living memory. An entry in the logbook of a Tiverton factory in April 1900 tells of the workers keeping 'high holiday' at the request of the mayor. 'For a first attempt, Tiverton's celebration of St George's Day was a gratifying success,' declared the writer of the log. 'Without distinctions of class or creed the inhabitants generally entered heartily into the festivities of the day.' The town was decorated with bunting and 'all business was concluded' by four o'clock to allow the celebrations to begin. After a small reception at the town hall, hosted by the mayor, a larger party was held also in the town hall, followed by 'fireworks on a scale superior to anything witnessed in the district since the Jubilee'.

Although the writer recorded that the event failed to raise as much money for the famine fund as officials had hoped for, he concluded that the social benefit had been immense and that the saint's day was to become an annual event. 'The celebration cannot fail to be of permanent benefit in the way of stimulating patriotism and intensifying interest in the Empire. Dwellers in the provinces have an inevitable tendency to take narrow views and become parochial. It is well now and then to be reminded that we belong to a race with a history, a heritage and a future.'

In her 1908 book *St George for Merrie England*, Margaret H Bulley lamented the passing of many traditional events but added, 'It is delightful, however, to find that even in these practical and prosaic times traces of old customs still linger in the country districts, reminding us of the old esteem and the old reverence. To this day boys on hobby horses parade some of the small Kentish villages on April 23, masquerading as St George, and no doubt reaping a few pennies for their pains.' She revealed, 'Until a few years ago an old ballad called *St George for England*, was sung at Windsor on April 23 by the choir boys of St George's Chapel, and from the time of George I until the reign of the late Queen Victoria, a golden rose decorated the royal dining-table, on the same day, the rose being the emblem of the Saint.'

At that time, according to Ms Bulley, the custom of wearing a rose on 23 April was still adhered to in England and the colonies.

CHAPTER EIGHT

Twentieth-Century Boy

There is a forgotten, nay almost forbidden word, which
means more to me than any other. That word is England.

WINSTON CHURCHILL

*W*here the Rainbow Ends, a novel by Mrs Clifford Mills,
gives an interesting insight into attitudes towards
St George in the early part of the twentieth century.
Published in 1911, with a cover that showed an armour-clad
St George surrounded by four blond children and a lion cub,
this very English work was soon adapted into a stage play
which was performed on an annual basis for years to come.
It focuses on two youngsters, children of the empire,
called Cris and Rosamund, who are left with an evil aunt and
uncle when their parents are lost at sea while returning from
India. After consulting the 'Rainbow Book', introduced to
them by a kindly cousin, they set off to find 'The Land
Where All Lost Loved Ones Are Found', beyond the realm of
the Dragon King. Granted two wishes each by a genie, Cris
asks for the help of his naval cadet buddy Blunders, while

Rosamund calls for the aid of a heroic knight, and names St George.

The man who appears before them is far from their vision of a knight in shining armour, but is instead an old grey-haired man. The reason for his decline, he reveals, is that he is an 'unemployed Ideal' – the English people have forgotten about him thanks to a trick played by the wicked Dragon King. When Rosamund tells him, 'I am an English maiden in danger,' and requests help, he changes once more into a handsome knight, 'golden-haired, blue-eyed, English of the English'.

The children are then captured by the Dragon King, tried and found guilty of placing themselves under the protection of an Ideal, the dragons' most dangerous enemies. St George, explains the king, is more dangerous than most because 'he alone can build about your country, England, a sure, impregnable defence – the wall of patriotism'. Sentenced to death, the children are saved after Cris makes a St George's flag from a white hanky and the red collar of his pet lion cub, prompting St George to appear and slay the Dragon King. The children are then reunited with their parents and returned to England, to live 'henceforth and forever in the hearts of children of his race'.

The tone of the story is disturbingly jingoistic and would be considered shockingly racist today. The man attempting to deprive the children of their home is a German Jew named Schnapps, and the genie is described as 'of Ethiopian darkness, but not at all repulsive looking'. However, the imperial aspect of the book and the idea that St George has grown old and useless through the neglect of the English people shows how far his cult had dropped out of favour and suggests it had become the preserve of the ruling classes.

SCOUTING FOR SAINTS

WHILE SETTING UP the Boy Scout movement in 1908 Sir Robert Baden-Powell, a national hero in his own right following the famous Siege of Mafeking, chose to adopt George as its patron saint. During the 217-day siege in South Africa eleven years earlier, Baden-Powell's troops had been surrounded by 8,000 Boer soldiers but through deceptions and bravery the British eventually prevailed. During the siege Baden-Powell had been impressed by the skills and resourcefulness of the young boys he used as scouts and he set about writing *Aids to Scouting,* which became widely used in the UK as a handbook for boys.

Encouraged, Baden-Powell wrote *Scouting for Boys,* the cornerstone for the modern Scout movement, which can now be found in over a hundred countries. However, at first he concentrated on English boys, who, he believed, should behave in a chivalrous and brave manner at all times. In the book he claimed that King Arthur and the Knights of the Round Table chose St George as their own patron. 'They had as their patron saint St George, because he was the only one of all the saints who was a horseman,' he wrote. 'He is the Patron Saint of cavalry from which the word Chivalry is derived, and the special saint of England. He is also the Patron Saint of Boy Scouts everywhere.'

Baden-Powell went on to tell the story of St George before concluding,

> When he was faced by a difficulty or danger, however great it appeared – even in the shape of a dragon – he did not avoid it or fear it, but went at it with all the power he could put into himself and his horse. Although inadequately armed for such an encounter, having merely a spear, he charged in, did his best, and finally succeeded in overcoming a difficulty which nobody had dared to tackle.
>
> That is exactly the way in which a Scout should face a difficulty or danger, no matter how great or terrifying it may appear to him or how ill-equipped he may be for the struggle.
>
> He should go at it boldly and confidently, using every power that he can to try to overcome it, and the probability is that he will succeed.

'B-P' decreed that on every 23 April, Scouts everywhere would remind themselves of their promise and of the Scout

Law, a tradition which survives today. Alice Brewster, an author writing specifically for the Scouts in 1914, backed up Baden-Powell's claim that the saint had inspired the Arthurian knights in her book *The Life of Saint George, the Patron Soldier-Saint of England.*

Many of the images produced by the Scout Association in its early days use St George as inspiration. One shows a healthy-looking Scout in front of a green curtain bearing the motto 'Be Prepared' rolling up his sleeves as if to get stuck into battle while gazing at a statue of the mounted St George. Sir Robert's 1920 book *Young Knights of the Empire* shows a young lad in armour holding a banner bearing the Red Cross, on which the title is printed. The boy guards a cage containing an extremely defeated-looking dragon, and 'Honour, God and the King', 'Obey the law of the Scouts' and 'Do a good turn to somebody every day' are engraved on the cage's bars.

St George's Day is still celebrated by Scouts, Guides and other associated organisations with parades and church services in England and in many other countries, including Germany, Russia, Hungary and the Ukraine.

WORLD WAR I

A S A FIGURE frequently used to represent chivalry in combat and military might, St George was bound to enjoy a peak in popularity during the dark days of war. Apart from the battlefield apparitions (*see pages 44–47*), the rallying calls of leaders echoed that of Henry V at Agincourt. One commanding officer, fighting in Zeebrugge on St George's Day 1918, was said to have announced the charge with the words 'St George for England! Let's twist the dragon's tail.'

Back in Britain, the figure of St George was being used to recruit soldiers. One poster printed in 1915, before conscription was introduced, showed the heroic knight on horseback, slaying a vicious dragon, with the words 'Britain Needs You At Once' along the top and bottom. Many newspaper cartoons produced during the Great War showed an impressive-looking saint overcoming the dragon, in a clear reference to the fight between good and evil, and some postcards of the era depicted his appearances to troops during the bloody conflict.

Unfortunately, the saint's name was taken in vain by the Germans. In one Western Front offensive, in March 1918, Ludendorff planned to attack the Allied troops in northern France in an operation codenamed Michael. Three other attacks which would back up the move were planned: St George I against the British on the Lys river, St Georges II against the front near Ypres, and Blücher against the French in Champagne. One prong of the attack, at Arras, proved successful, but the British resisted the advance of the German troops admirably elsewhere in what became know as the Second Battle of the Somme.

British victory in the war led inevitably to a resurgence in George's popularity, with memorial works frequently taking his form. The most famous of these is the Cavalry Memorial, which now stands at Hyde Park Corner in London.

Designed by Adrian Jones, it is a magnificent statue of St George on horseback in full armour, slaying a serpent-like dragon. A broken lance can be seen in the neck of the beast as St George lifts his arm aloft in a triumphant salute. The bronze figure was cast from captured guns and the armour was modelled on an effigy of the Earl of Warwick, cast in 1454. The memorial, which originally stood at Stanhope Gate, was unveiled by Field Marshall Earl of Ypres in May 1924 and commemorative plaques to further cavalry casualties were added after World War II.

A further memorial in the image of the saint, sculpted by C L Hartwell, can be found at St John's Wood parish church and a replica of this serves as a monument to the fallen of Newcastle. At St James's Catholic church, Spanish Place, in London's Marylebone a chapel dedicated to those who gave their lives in the conflict is adorned with three stained-glass windows, featuring St George, St Michael and the Virgin Mary, representing the army, the air force and the navy. George is standing over a slain green dragon while Michael triumphs over a similar monster of red.

WORLD WAR II

T HE HELPFUL SPECTRE of St George, ever present on the battlefields of the First World War, seems to have deserted the soldiers of the Second, as no apparitions were reported. As we have seen, however, King George VI sought to involve the saint in the conflict with the creation of the George Cross and the George Medal, for acts of bravery by civilians (*see pages 47–48*). Actor Sir Laurence Olivier also did his bit with a film of Shakespeare's *Henry V*. Partly financed by the British government, the movie was intended as a propaganda exercise to boost morale in the dark days of war. Interestingly, during the war the Russians made use of the soldier saint. One anti-fascist poster shows a Russian soldier killing a huge serpent in the shape of a swastika and many war memorials depict St George, who is also the patron saint of Russia.

POST-WAR PATRON

THE BREAK-UP of the British empire in the years following World War II left St George increasingly side-lined. With British society becoming ever more multicultural, the flag-waving patriotism associated with England's patron saint began to look at best old-fashioned and at worst xenophobic. Both the flag and the name of the saint were sadly hijacked by far right groups such as the League of St George. This neo-Nazi organisation was set up in 1974 as a breakaway from the Action Party formed by the British fascist Oswald Mosley. Not only did the doctrine of the league state that 'racial solidarity' should be encouraged and that only the 'folk' of the country should be 'entitled to nationality and citizen-ship in their own land', they also denounced feminism as a 'left-wing cult' a stance which spelled the end of chivalry.

The modern-day British National Party has also led images of the red cross and England's patron saint to be associated with racism rather than patriotism. The party opposes immigration and calls for 'voluntary resettlement' of immigrants already in the UK. A recent leaflet from the organisation, emblazoned with an image of the saint on a rearing horse against a red cross, urged the country to

'Celebrate St George and campaign for an English Parliament.' 'The establishment hate the English,' the leaflet reads. 'While everybody else's special days are celebrated – often with our taxes – St George and the English are despised and forgotten.' The fact that their chosen patron was a Turkish-born soldier who the BNP would see thrown out of the country should he set foot on English shores today seems to have escaped them.

Declining interest in the saint was not helped by the announcement in May 1969 that the Roman Catholic Church had downgraded his St George's Day to an optional local festival, although it was to keep its full feast day status in England, as befits a country's patron. Yet, apart from the Scouts, Guides and the small patriotic societies, there were few people celebrating the event.

As the century came to a close, two events were to revive interest in the near-moribund saint. The first was England's hosting of the football tournament Euro '96, which saw an abundance of red and white flags all over the country and opened with a lively pageant featuring St George slaying a huge animatronic dragon surrounded by actors in brightly coloured medieval dress. The second was devolution. The Scotland Act and the Government of Wales Act in 1998 led to calls for England to stand up for its own identity, just as the other three nations of Great Britain were doing. As the country moved into the twenty-first-century, many felt it was time to reclaim England's patron saint.

FAR FROM SAINTLY SITCOM

THE DRAGON LEGEND lent its name to a risqué comedy starring Sid James and Peggy Mount in the 1960s. *George and the Dragon* followed the sexual adventures of a lecherous chauffeur whose exploits had seen off sixteen housekeepers at the home of Colonel Maynard, played by John Le Mesurier. The seventeenth, the aptly named Miss Gabriel Dragon, is a belligerent battleaxe who has no time for George's shenanigans. He decides to get rid of her by pretending to have the hots for her, but she scuppers every scheme he hatches. The black-and-white sitcom was a huge success and ran for twenty-six episodes between 1966 and 1968.

CHAPTER NINE

The Red Cross

ENGLAND'S ASSOCIATION with the red cross flag dates back to the twelfth century, but when the banner was adopted, and why, is in some dispute. One widely held view is that the flag belonged to the city of Genoa first, and was flown by English ships sailing in the Mediterranean from 1190 for protection. Pirates were a common problem at the time and it was not unusual for ships from one country to sail under the banner of another for security and tax reasons. The maritime republic of Genoa, which also claimed George as its patron saint, had one of the most powerful fleets in the world, rivalled in the region only by Venice. For the protection the flag gave ships registered in the City of London, the English monarch paid an annual fee to the doge of Genoa.

Another possible origin goes back one hundred years before that to the crusaders who are often pictured wearing a red cross on a white background. But this symbol of holy war was not exclusive to the English, nor was it linked to St George. In November 1095 Pope Urban II appealed to Christian monarchs to band together against the Muslim domination of the Middle East. At the Council of Clermont he told the gathered knights and noblemen, 'Men of God, men chosen and blessed among all, combine your forces! Take the road to the Holy Sepulchre assured of the imperishable glory that awaits you in God's kingdom. Let each one deny himself and take the Cross!' His audience responded with the shout 'God wills it!' and sprang into action.

They immediately chose a red cross on a white field as their emblem – red representing valour with white denoting purity – and the locality sold out of red material within hours. The knights cut up the fabric and had crossed strips sewn onto their sleeves, thus earning themselves the name crusaders, from the Latin *crux* meaning cross. When the united armies went into battle, they wore huge red crosses on their tabards, regardless of country or rank, and this was soon added to flags and banners. Later in the crusades, however, the various nationalities used different ensigns, and it seems that the English wore a white cross on a red background. Historian Professor Joshua Prawer, in his 1988 book *A History of the Latin Kingdom of Jerusalem*, claims that Henry II and France's Philip II met under an old tree at Gisors on the Normandy border in January 1188, where 'the two rivals agreed to stop the wars between them and swear to "take the cross". They also agreed to establish symbols to the different corps: [a] white cross for the Plantagenet corps of Henry II, a red cross for the Capetian corps of Phillip II, and a green cross for the Flemish.'

The unsubstantiated theory is that the two countries then swapped colours around 1400, with France later opting to change its background again, to dark blue. It is possible, though, that stories of St George's helpful appearances at the crusades (*see pages 34–35*) led to his being associated with the red cross, and the two ideals being adopted by the English together. The earliest images of St George often showed him in armour but without any sign of a red cross. The tympanum at Fordington, *c.*1100 (*see page 51*) shows St George in battle, holding a lance with a banner on which a cross can be seen. This would have been shortly after the apparition at Antioch and therefore very much linked to the crusades. To the Christian world, the crusaders were fighting a just and holy war, defending Christianity, just as St George had during both his martyrdom and the battle against the dragon. Medieval depictions began to link the two by showing the saint with a white tabard decorated with a red cross over his suit of armour even before the flag was adopted by the English.

The first record of the red cross being used as a military ensign by an English army is at the Battle of Evesham in 1265, where forces loyal to Henry III fought under the banner, although association with St George was not the primary reason. The flag was chosen as the direct opposite of the white cross against a red background used by the rebel barons under Simon De Montfort. In 1277 Edward I was the first English king to display the red cross on the battlefield as a sign of St George.

During the Hundred Years War, from 1337 to 1453, the cross of St George became the flag of the English military, particularly in the reign of Henry V. As well as invoking the saint at the Battle of Agincourt in 1415 (*see pages 41–42*), the king ordered the banner to be raised over the town gates when his army captured Harfleur. By this time, the cross of St George already featured in the arms of many towns and cities, including London. The figure of the city's patron St Paul holding the sword which symbolised his martyrdom was replaced with the cross of St George, with St Paul's sword in the first quarter. In 1381 mayor William Walworth ordered changes to the mayoral seal so that the figures of St Paul and Thomas à Becket, which were already present, now stood above a cross of St George supported by lions. In the fifteenth century the coat of arms acquired two dragons which further reinforced George's claim on the image, as well as the motto '*Domine dirige nos*' – 'Lord, guide us.' The Reformation in the sixteenth century led to the cross becoming firmly established as the English National flag, as all other saints' emblems were banned by law. The earliest record of the cross of St George flying at sea, as the flag of England with no other saintly flags, was 1545.

UNION JACK

O**N THE DEATH** of Elizabeth I in 1603, the Scottish king James VI inherited the kingdom of England, which included Ireland and Wales, and was crowned James I of England on 25 July 1603. The union of the countries meant a new flag was deemed necessary and in 1606 the new design was specified by royal proclamation. 'All our subjects in this our isle and kingdom of Great Britain and the members thereof, shall bear in their main top the red cross commonly called St George's Cross and the white cross commonly called St Andrew's Cross joined together according to a form made by our heralds and sent to our Admiral to be published to our said subjects.' However, the first flag of Great Britain was only to be used on ships, and hence became known as the Union Jack, a jack being a standard flown on the bow of a vessel. In 1634 its use was restricted further by Charles I, who decreed that only royal ships could display it. On land English forces still fought under the cross of St George. The new design formed the basis of today's Union flag, although the Irish St Patrick's cross wasn't incorporated until 1801.

The 1606 flag met with a great deal of disapproval, not least from the Scots, who objected to St Andrew's cross being overlaid by the flag of England. Encouraged by John Erskine, earl of Mar, a large group of Scotsmen sent a letter to the Privy Council of Scotland, to be passed on to the king, which stated that the flag's design 'will breid some heit [heat] and miscontentment betwix your Majesties subjectis, and it is to be feirit [feared] that some inconvenientis sail [shall] fall oute betwix thame, for our seyfaring men cannot be inducit to resave that flage as it is set down'. Alternative designs were put forward by the Scots but none was adopted. It is possible, however, that some among the king's Scottish subjects flew an unofficial flag which gave their national symbol more prominence as during a royal visit to Dumfries in 1617 the town commissar was reported to have stated, 'Your Royall Majestie, in whose sacred person the King of kings hath miraculouslie united so many glorious Kingdoms, under whose Scepter the whyte and reid crocies are so proportionablie interlaced.' In his *Story of Scotland's Flag* Paul Harris backs up the theory of the unofficial Scottish version with the observation that in 1693 John Slezer, captain of artillery and surveyor-general of stores and magazines in Scotland, produced an engraving of Edinburgh Castle in which a flag is shown with the St Andrew's cross overlying that of St George.

The passion felt by the Scots on the issue of Scotland's union with England was often demonstrated by satirical writings which compared patron saints. One such poem, 'A Comparison Between St Andrew and St George' was written in 1634.

The Red Crosses, in people or in priest,

Was a foule marke upon a Scottish breist,

St Andrew is for Men, St George for clownes.[8]

Despite the prominence of St George's cross on the Union Jack, there was also some dissent among the English, who objected to it being adulterated at all. Before the final design was decreed in 1606, various alternatives were mooted including the two flags sitting side by side in one larger one, and another which had the cross of St George in all its glory with a tiny St Andrew's cross in the first white quarter – hardly a model to go down well north of the Border.

In 1707 the Acts of Union by the English and Scottish parliaments officially created the United Kingdom of Great Britain. Shortly before this momentous event, seven designs for the Union flag were submitted to the monarch, Queen Anne, and her privy council by the appropriately named Sir Henry St George. One of the designs was the 'Scottish Union Flag' which had St Andrew's cross overlying the cross of St George. Not surprisingly, the largely English privy council rejected this design and plumped for a similar version to the 1606 flag. This then became 'the ensign armorial of the United Kingdom of Great Britain' as one of the provisions of the Acts of Union.

In 1801, a year after another Act of Union joined Ireland

8. Samantha Riches, *St George: Hero, Martyr and Myth.*

to Great Britain to form the United Kingdom, a red saltire (diagonal cross), was added to represent St Patrick. Irish nationalists, however, rejected the association of this symbol with their patron saint as a convenient invention of the British.

DUNKIRK JACK

IN MAY 1940 thousands of Allied troops were trapped and under attack from the German military on the French beaches, sustaining huge casualties. Vice Admiral Michael Ray Kern called for all available boats to sail to Dunkirk in a huge rescue operation. Over 700 lifeboats, civilian and merchant craft responded to the call, and over the course of nine days their crews risked life and limb to evacuate 338,226 English and French soldiers from the shores of France. The 'little ships of Dunkirk' were rewarded with the right to fly the St George's cross from their bows. This became known as the Dunkirk Jack, and the only other ships permitted to fly this flag are those which have an admiral of the fleet on board.

THE FOOTBALL FACTOR

A T ANY SPORTS EVENT involving an England team, from football and rugby to cricket and even tennis, the crowd is now awash with red and white flags and faces painted with the cross of St George. A visitor to the country may assume that this has always been the case but the reclaiming of St George's flag for the majority of English sports fans is a relatively new thing, going back to the patriotic fervour created by Euro '96. England's hosting of the UEFA football tournament for the first time led to a profusion of red and white flags appearing in suburban gardens, hung from flat windows and trailing from cars. The flag was once more a symbol of English endeavour, albeit on the sports field rather than the battlefield, and it soon became a fixture among England supporters of all sports. In 2005, after the England cricket team regained the Ashes amid a sea of red and white cloth, songwriter and commentator Billy Bragg, writing in the *Daily Mirror,* was delighted to see that the English had 'reclaimed our own flag'.

Watching the crowd in Trafalgar Square celebrating the Ashes win, I couldn't help but be amazed at how quickly the flag of

St George has replaced the Union Jack in the affections of England fans.

A generation ago, England games looked a lot like Last Night of the Proms, with the red, white and blue firmly to the fore. Now, it seems, the English have begun to remember who they are.

This new development in the national identity, he believed, was traceable to the 1996 Wembley tournament, where 'When the Scots came to Wembley, England fans were suddenly made aware that, no matter how attached to it they felt, the Union Jack wasn't actually their flag. It belonged to the British.' The solution was clear. The cross of St George was back.

CHAPTER TEN

St George Today

A recent survey carried out by *This England* magazine found that seven out of ten young people in England didn't know the date of St George's Day, and other studies have shown that more than a quarter of those living in the country have no idea who their patron saint is. Perhaps even more shocking is the fact that St Patrick's Day, 17 March, is more likely to be marked in the streets and pubs of the country than our own saint's feast.

Yet evidence that St George has not been totally forgotten can be found in towns and cities throughout England, particularly in the numerous churches and pubs that bear his name. A stroll through London will take you past many a church dedicated to him, both Catholic and Protestant, including the magnificent St George's cathedral, mother church of the Catholic archdiocese of Southwark.

Villages such as Wrotham in Kent have often taken St George as a theme which extends from the church to the primary school and the pub, usually called the George and

Dragon, as well as featuring on the village sign. In all there are 138 pubs called the George and Dragon in England, and many more known as the George, although whether these are named after the saint is often in doubt. 'The George can refer to the saint or one of our Hanoverian kings,' comments Alan Rose of the Inn Sign Society. 'It's a very blurred area. You can sometimes tell by the age of the building, so if it's an old wattle-and-daub structure, it is probably named after St George. But even a modern 1930s pub, which you might assume was named after the king, could be built on the site of an original pub named after the saint.'

St George-Related Pub Names

138	George & Dragon	10	Royal George Hotel
118	George Hotel	9	St Georges Hotel
113	George	7	Old George
92	George Inn	6	George & Dragon Hotel
38	Royal George	5	St George
13	George IV	5	St Georges Tavern
10	George & Dragon Inn		

© CGA Outlet Index Dec 2009

THE RIGHT ON HIS SIDE

Pubs and churches aside, one of the problems St George has suffered in the modern era is the association of his cult, particularly his flag, with the far right. The British National Party has long used the symbolism as its own, and because of this it is often seen as menacing in an increasingly multi-cultural society. A survey for *New Nation* magazine discovered that 'most black people interviewed said they felt alienated by the flag of St George and still associated it with the BNP'. The study for *This England* also found that one in eight people found it embarrassing to see a St George's cross flying, due to the symbol having been hijacked by extremists. The association with racism became so entrenched that in 2003 Rugby Borough Council caused a storm when they voted against flying the flag over the town hall throughout the year on the grounds that it would 'send out the wrong messages'.

'It is time that St George was reclaimed from the dragon, from past associations with racism and the far Right,' says Simon Barrow, author of a 2007 report in the *Church of England Newspaper*. His cry was one of many gathering momentum among the people of England.

RECLAIMING THE SAINT

I N THE YEAR 2000, the Catholic Church, which had relegated the saint's day to the lowest category of memorial, reinstated it as a proper feast day. At the same time calls for St George's Day to be recognised as a significant event were growing.

In 2005 in *Time Out* magazine Billy Bragg called for the saint to be venerated by the populace of England once more and mourned the fact that 'Sadly St George's Day conjures up the negative image of the beer-bellied, shaven-headed lout setting his bull terrier on an asylum seeker. The great irony is that St George himself was an immigrant.' He concluded that the saint was a great patron to have in a multicultural society, precisely because his origins were not English. 'This olive-skinned stranger from the Middle East might help us slay the dragon of English xenophobia.'

That same year, on 23 April, cricket legend Ian Botham delivered a petition to 10 Downing Street calling for St George's Day to be made a national holiday. The petition was signed by more than 527,000 people and the former England batsman was passionate in his argument. 'Why shouldn't it be a national holiday?' he was quoted as saying in the *Daily Express*.

Our heritage is being eroded. Large numbers of people do not know anything about St George and yet we see the flag raised at cricket and football grounds.

My message is that people should be proud to be English, supporting the patron saint – that seems obvious to me, every other country would – and English products.

To mark the occasion, plates of roast beef were handed out to visitors and workers at the headquarters of the three main political parties and a poll voted George Harrison the greatest George of all time.

Sadly, not everyone appeared to be behind the rallying cry, as landlord Tony Bennett found out in 2005. He was appalled when his application for an extended licence for a St George's Day celebration, at his Otter pub, in Drayton near Norwich, was turned down on the grounds that in the eyes of the law it was not 'a special day'. Yet he had been granted a late licence for Chinese New Year. 'We no longer celebrate our country in the way others do. We need a day for the English.'

Two years later, the Church of England took up the cause with the aforementioned report in its newspaper. 'The patron saint of England should be rebranded and St George's Day should become a national day to celebrate the tradition of dissent,' said the report. A simultaneous article in the *Morning Advertiser*, magazine of the licensed trade, called for the help of landlords everywhere. 'Licensees are asked to ring their bell at

10.45 p.m. on April 23 and ask customers to raise their glasses in a grand toast to St George.'

Writing in the *Daily Telegraph*, Adam Edwards observed, 'The enthusiasm for Englishmen to proclaim St George's Day a national holiday is building. A ground swell of patriotism is returning after years of paying no heed to our avenging paragon while tolerating our Celtic neighbours' over-enthusiasm for nailing up griffins, wearing tartan and the lauding of little green men.' In the same edition, Irish writer Judith Woods urged the English to celebrate with a party, as her own compatriots did.

> So St George's Day once again looms darkly on the horizon, hovering menacingly like a guilty conscience. In any other country on the planet, there would be parades, piñatas, and the Chicago River would be dyed green. Even the Welsh, barely three million strong, can drum up enough daffodils and choirs to bring a tear to the eye of a prop forward.
>
> Not the English. Your interminable hand-wringing about whether or not to celebrate your patron saint's day presents further proof (if proof were needed) that England's self-esteem is on a long, drawn out slow puncture.

In recent years, however, there has been a steady move towards the celebration of the day, with red and white bunting appearing outside pubs and local celebrations in some parts of the country. Restaurants offer special menus featuring traditional dishes and local ingredients and even supermarkets have begun to promote special English products to mark the day.

In 2006 a private member's bill was tabled in the House of Commons by Andrew Rosindell which sought to make St George's Day a national holiday but it didn't receive enough backing to go any further. Two years later, the same MP posted an early-day motion which stated,

> That this House looks forward to celebrating St George's Day on Wednesday 23rd April; believes that the day of England's patron saint is an opportunity for all the people of England to celebrate their country's heritage, values and traditions; calls upon the Government to mark the occasion by ensuring that the Cross of St George flag is flown from all public buildings on this day; further encourages local authorities, schools, organisations and businesses also proudly to fly the flag of England; and further calls upon all hon. Members to support the campaign to establish 23rd April as an annual public holiday so that the people of England may be united in celebrating their country's great achievements and rich history.

Kent man Tim Allard made headlines when he became one of the first employers to give his staff the day off, in 2006, and he's been observing St George's Day ever since. 'There's a great movement now for taking St George's day off, having a public holiday and celebrating it,' he told local radio Invicta FM. 'And if it's not going to come from the top down it's got to come from the bottom up. As an employer I'm in a position to make it happen for my folks so that's what we've done. I think it's becoming increasingly important because, without becoming too political, we do seem to be losing our English identity. He went on to say he would like to start a trend among employers and hoped they would 'scratch their heads and think it's a good idea and follow suit'.

Even the social networking sites have got in on the act, proving that celebrating St George needn't be the preserve of the older generation. At the last count the Facebook group, Make St George's Day a Bank Holiday, has 12,255 fans and was growing all the time. One post read, 'I think it's an outrage that everyone remembers St Patrick's Day but everyone forgets St George's Day . . . let's make it a bank holiday so no one forgets and sod anyone that gets offended by it!!!' Young people on the MySpace website taking part in a recent survey agreed they should have a day off to celebrate St George but also nominated comedian Stephen Fry as a replacement patron saint! In 2009 the website stgeorgesday.com reported that their online petition, which called for the feast day to be made a national holiday, had over a million supporters.

As the Foreword to this book shows, London mayor Boris Johnson is a keen advocate of celebrating the feast day of the saint and in April 2009 he announced that the day would be celebrated with various events throughout London, including a free concert in Trafalgar Square. David Blunkett MP joined forces with Billy Bragg in 2005 to campaign for the day to be marked with special celebrations, and in a lecture entitled 'A New England: An English Identity Within Britain', which he gave to the Insitute of Public Policy Research in March of that year, he said, 'Nobody argues against celebrating St Patrick, St Andrew or St David – for many it is a chance to share in each other's traditions. Let us hope that a similar spirit can be found on St George's Day.' Being proud to be English, he argued, should not detract from being British or part of the European Union. Reflecting on the English identity he concluded,

> The English have always been diverse and outward-looking. We are an open, trading and enterprising people who have travelled the world and given it great science, literature and sport. We can have pride in ourselves and confidence in our future – building outwards from our localities, to a sense of Englishness as part of a United Kingdom and wider European Union.

The 'sense of Englishness' appears to be on the increase. According to data from the British Social Attitude surveys, when asked about their national identity in 1992 just 31 per cent of English people responded by saying they were English. In 2003 this had risen to 40 per cent. Again, in 1997 just 24 per cent of people when asked about their national identity said that they were either 'English' or 'more English than British'. This had risen to 36 per cent by 2003.

When England played Belarus at Wembley in October 2009, the enthusiastic crowd showed their backing for the England 2018 World Cup bid in spectacular style. Some 25,000 fans held up red and white cards to spell out 2018 in the south stand and form two huge crosses of St George at either end of the stadium.

In his book *Tickling the English* Irish comedian Dara O'Briain explained why he thought St George's Day would never be as popular as St Patrick's Day. 'You can't gobble up other nations, absorb them into your flag, and then whine that your original flag doesn't get enough attention,' he wrote. 'All this crying over the St George's flag is like a fat girl who ate everyone's cake wailing that she can't fit into her party dress any more. This is what you wanted with the empire, suck it up.'

CHAPTER ELEVEN

Celebrating St George

Prepared and alert a Scout follows the lead
Of our Patron St George and his spirited steed.

SIR ROBERT BADEN-POWELL

A S WELL AS pub and restaurant celebrations, there has been a return to more traditional methods of observing St George's Day in recent years. Many cities throughout the country have annual processions, with local associations and members of the community dressing in costumes and parading through the streets on floats.

One of the biggest and most famous of the annual marches takes place at Sandwell in the West Midlands. Sadly, this peaceful march almost lost its local funding in 2009 after right wing extremists hijacked the event. Members of the BNP were seen among the 15,000 revellers the year before and the council initially voted to withdraw funding. The organisers fought back and Councillor Bill Thomas announced in March that the decision had been overturned. 'Sandwell Council has a proud tradition of celebrating St George's Day,' he said. 'We are fully committed to it and will be spending more than £38,000 on celebrating this special day.'

On the day, however, the row broke out again when BNP leader Nick Griffin and deputy leader Simon Darby turned up. 'I'm here as an Englishman, not to be party political,' claimed Griffin, but Councillor Derek Rowley countered, 'Clearly the parade has been infiltrated by right wing extremists and they were bound to say they weren't being political.'

Most parades in England are less controversial, however, and are steeped in tradition and fun. Since Sir Robert Baden-Powell chose the saint as a figurehead for the Scouts and, a year later, the Guides, both these organisations and their spin-off groups, such as the Cubs, Brownies and Rangers, have been the mainstay of St George's Day parades throughout England and countries around the world, including Canada, Russia and the Ukraine. Every year hundreds of Scouts and Guides are invited to the annual parade at Windsor Castle, attended by the queen or another senior member of the royal family. Other historic attractions which host their own celebrations include Richmond Castle, on the River Swale, where storytellers often regale the crowd with the life of St George, and Kenilworth Castle, where a St George in full armour traditionally defeats his dragon. At Cressing Temple in Essex the Templars are remembered with a jousting match.

MUMMERS

Although mumming plays have probably been acted for centuries the first known scripts only date back as far as 1779. The central characters are always St George, also called King George, and an evil Persian king with whom he must do battle. In many plays, such as the Lutterworth St George play published in 1865, another character known as the doctor revives the saint after he perishes at the hands of his enemy. This is thought to refer to St Michael who, according to one version of the legend, resurrects George after his martyrdom. However, some mumming plays also include the figures of the dragon and, drawing on Richard Johnson's rather English legend, the beautiful Princess Sabra. These probably originate from a Cornish script by William Sandys, published in 1833.

Although the plays were performed through England, Ireland and Europe in the 1800s, Margaret Bulley's 1908 book *St George for Merrie England* refers to them as being a speciality of 'the children of North-country villages on Christmas Eve, where, among a strange medley of characters, we again meet our old friends St George, Sabra, the Sultan of Egypt, and the dragon.' Bulley then quotes the opening lines.

O here comes I St George a man of Courage Bold
And with my spear I winnd three crowns of gold.
I slew the dragon, and brought him to the slaughter,
And by that means I married Sabra, the beauteous
   King of Egypt's daughter.

Many believe the term mummer comes from the Old English word mum, meaning silence, suggesting the plays were originally performed as mimes. Others believe the word comes from the Greek *mommo*, meaning mask.

MORRIS DANCING

ALTHOUGH Morris dancing is traditionally linked with May Day, the dancers are always out in force on St George's Day as part of the celebration of all things English. The men and women, whose customary dress involves braces, hats and bells, dance in groups and use props such as sticks and handkerchiefs, but there is some evidence that the routines occasionally used to involve a dragon, in a clear reference to the patron saint. There are three main types of Morris dancers: Cotswold Morris dancers use hankies and sticks; North West Morris dancers wear clogs and have a more military style; and Border Morris dancers, from the Welsh border, who blacken or paint their faces.

RAISING A GLASS

ENGLAND's celebrations of its patron saint are inextricably linked to the most English of tipples, real ale. Just as St Patrick's Day means sales of Guinness soar, an Englishman will toast the honourable dragon slayer with a pint of bitter. A recent survey by the website This is London found that 48 per cent of those asked thought real ale should be the official St George's Day drink. The runners up were lager (19 per cent), Babycham (17 per cent), cider (9 per cent), snakebite[9] (5 per cent) and eggnog (2 per cent).

A spokesman for the Campaign for Real Ale, which supports the celebration of St George's Day in pubs across the country, commented, 'Real ale truly is the drink of choice for patriotic English men and women. You can forget your fizzy foreign lagers and sugary alcopops and support St George's Day with a traditional pint of English real ale.' Young's Brewery in Wandsworth used to produce a bottled beer named after the saint, which featured the English flag and a picture of George slaying the dragon on the label.

---

9. A cocktail of equal parts cider and lager, sometimes sweetened with a dash of blackcurrant cordial.

CHAPTER TWELVE

St George in Literature

S T GEORGE has cropped up in many a literary tale throughout history, quite apart from the fanciful retellings of his story in the Middle Ages. In 1589 Edmund Spenser published the first book of his epic poem *The Faerie Queene*, which, with the second book published seven years later, is the longest poem in the English language. The work was intended as a tribute to Elizabeth I, and the original plan, outlined in a letter to Sir Walter Raleigh, was to include twenty-four stories, although the format changed before completion. The poem, which pleased the queen so much that she granted Spenser a pension of fifty pounds a year, was split into six parts, each extolling a Christian value. The first book, 'Holiness', had a character called the Redcrosse Knight as its hero in a clear reference to St George.

This 'Gentle Knight' wears a red cross on a white background and travels on horseback accompanied by a 'Ladie' of royal blood named Una, who keeps a lamb on a lead. This is a reference to the dragon-slaying tale and the princess who escaped the beast's jaws. Spenser describes the knight's cross and later names him as the true St George.

> And on his brest a bloodie cross he bore,
> The deare remembrance of his dying Lord,
> For whose sweete sake that glorious badge he wore,
> And dead, as living, ever he ador'd.
> Upon his shield the like was also scor'd
> For soveraine hope which in his helpe he had.

After slaying one creature, which is half snake, half woman, the knight, in dented armour, travels across a barren plain to fight another dragon in a bloody three-day battle during which he is close to death three times but is revived through miracles, just as the real saint was during his martyrdom. With the beast finally vanquished, the chivalrous knight rescues her parents, marries Una and continues to pledge his allegiance to the queen. The Redcrosse Knight is linked to King Arthur, who embodies the chivalric values of all heroes. He is also portrayed as a champion of Gloriana, the Faerie Queene, who represents Queen Elizabeth I.

Another work designed to please the Virgin Queen was written by Gerard de Malynes and published in 1601. In *St George for England, Allegorically Described* the monarch was said to be the embodiment of St George himself.

For whereas under the person of the noble champion St George our saviour Christ was prefigured, delivering the Virgin (which did signify the sinful souls of Christians) from the dragon or devil's power; so her most excellent majesty by advancing the pure doctrine of Christ Jesus in all truth and sincerity, hath (as an instrument appointed by divine providence) been used to perform the part of a valiant champion.

THE BARD AND THE SAINT

I see you stand like greyhounds in the slips,
Straining upon the start. The game's afoot:
Follow your spirit; and, upon this charge,
Cry 'God for Harry! England and St George!'

Henry V's famous speech at Agincourt in Shakespeare's epic play is perhaps the only St George quote that readily springs to the lips. But the saint is mentioned once more in the Bard's lesser-known *King John:* 'St George that swinged the dragon and e'er since / Sits on his horse back at mine hostess' door.' The most English of writers, Shakespeare is irrevocably linked to the saint through his birth and death days supposedly both falling on 23 April, in 1564 and 1616. This convenient and satisfying patriotic coincidence, however, may not be entirely accurate. We know that he was baptised on 26 April but the date of his actual birth is not documented.

PILGRIM'S PROGRESS

JOHN BUNYAN's most famous work, published in two parts in 1679 and 1684, is an allegory concerning the defence of Christian beliefs against the authorities. It was begun by the author as he served a jail sentence for preaching outside a registered church, an activity banned in 1664. The main character, Christian, may well have been modelled on St George as he battles a dragon known as Apollyon, meaning destruction. The fight lasts half a day and ends when Christian wounds the beast with a double-edged sword 'And with that Apollyon spread his dragon wings and sped away.'

IVANHOE

SIR WALTER SCOTT mentions St George frequently in his famous novel, written in 1819 but set in the twelfth century. The title character, Wilfred of Ivanhoe, identifies himself with St George throughout the book. As he defends the Jewess Rebecca, he is challenged by a herald, who demands his rank, name and purpose. He replies,

> I am a good knight and noble, come hither to sustain with lance and sword the just and lawful quarrel of this damsel, Rebecca, daughter of Isaac of York; to uphold the doom pronounced against her to be false and truthless, and to defy Sir Brian de Bois-Guilbert, as a traitor, murderer, and liar; as I will prove in this field with my body against his, by the aid of God, of Our Lady, and of Monseigneur St George, the good knight.

But it is not only good and true knights who invoke the national saint. At one point Ivanhoe's father and travelling companions are assailed by kidnappers posing as Saxon bandits, who rally their accomplices with shouts of 'A white dragon! A white dragon! St George for merry England!' The same cry is repeated by the Saxons during a battle against the

Normans, while it is reworded during the storming of the castle by Robin Locksley, aka Robin Hood, who leads his men on with, 'St George! Merry St George for England! To the charge, bold yeomen!'

U A FANTHORPE

INSPIRED BY the famous painting of St George and the dragon by Paolo Uccello, which hangs in the National Gallery, British poet U A Fanthorpe (1929–2009) wrote a witty triptych called *Not My Best Side*. Written from the standpoints of the three protagonists, it starts with the dragon complaining that the artist had not given him time to pose properly and goes on:

> Poor chap, he had this obsession with
> Triangles, so he left off two of my
> Feet. I didn't comment at the time
> (What, after all, are two feet
> To a monster?)

The princess, he moans, was too unattractive to be edible and the amount of blood spilled in the painting is too little, showing he wasn't taken seriously.

The princess, in turn, bemoans the fact that she rather

liked the dragon, and objected to being rescued by a man in 'machinery' whose face she couldn't see.

> He might have acne, blackheads or even
> Bad breath for all I could tell.

However, she concedes that she must choose the victor because 'a girl's got to think of her future'.

Finally, we hear St George boasting, 'I have diplomas in Dragon Management and Virgin Reclamation,' before describing his horse as 'the latest model, with Automatic transmission and built-in obsolescence' and his armour as 'still on the secret list'. He then argues that the pair before him should be grateful to be killed/ rescued in the most modern way and tells them their objections are endangering jobs in the 'spear and horse-building industry'. Eventually he concludes that it doesn't matter what they want, they are in his way and he will do what his legend decrees.

This work helped launch Fanthorpe's career when it was published in 1978 in her first book *Side Effects*.

MODERN LITERATURE

THE CHARACTERS of the St George legend rarely feature in adult literature in the modern era, although the occasional romance, such as *St George and the Dragon* by Beth Andrews, uses ideas of medieval chivalry. Andrews has two lads, Richard St George and Julian Marchmount, embarking on a quest to romance mysterious young ladies locked away in a Gothic abbey. However, in recent years there have been many retellings of the saint's battle with the dragon in children's picture books. Some junior novels have also taken up the idea of a modern equivalent of the patron saint. *The Saint of Dragons* by Jason Hightman has a main character called Simon St George, who discovers he is a descendant of the real thing and there are still dragons, disguised as powerful humans, that he must defeat.

In *Dracula*, Bram Stoker suggested that St George's Day was like a modern-day Halloween, when evil is let loose on the world. He did, however give the date as 5 May, the date on the Gregorian calendar that the Eastern Orthodox Church celebrated it. In 1897, when the book was written, there were twelve days between the Gregorian and Julian calendars as opposed to the thirteen there are today.

'Do you know what day it is?' I answered that it was the fourth of May. She shook her head as she said again: 'Oh, yes! I know that, I know that! but do you know what day it is?' On my saying that I did not understand, she went on: 'It is the eve of St George's Day. Do you not know that tonight, when the clock strikes midnight, all the evil things in the world will have full sway?

CHAPTER THIRTEEN

St George in Art

THE EARLIEST images of St George appear in cycles, series of pictures which tell a whole story. Over a hundred such cycles, produced from the twelfth to the sixteenth century, still exist in Europe and, as many predate the dragon legend, they are primarily concerned with George's torture and death. The most famous of these appear in the Bedford Hours, created in France in 1423 to mark the wedding of the Duke of Bedford. Altar pieces and wall paintings were also a favourite way of depicting the martyrdom and, of the hundred or so known medieval frescoes featuring the saint created in England, over half can still be seen.

Later paintings, particularly in the Pre-Raphaelite style, almost exclusively depict his battle with the dragon.

THE BEDFORD HOURS

THIS FIFTEENTH-CENTURY manuscript, now kept in the British Library, marked the wedding of John of Lancaster, duke of Bedford and regent of France, to Anne, the daughter of the Duke of Burgundy. The work features an elaborate portrait of the duke kneeling before St George surrounded by five images of his torture. In the first the saint is naked on horseback being beaten with sticks; the second sees him tied to a saltire cross; in the third two torturers prepare to cut him in half with a two-handed saw; in the fourth he is placed in a cauldron. The final image, which stands alone in the top right-hand corner, shows him being thrown head first down a well.

ALABASTER RETABLES

TWO NOTABLE medieval carvings, made from alabaster quarried in the English Midlands in the 1480s, were commissioned for the altars of La Selle in Normandy and Borbjerg in Denmark. The Borbjerg retable, possibly commissioned in England to honour the patron saint of the nearby town of Holstebro, may not be entirely complete as it could well have been dismantled during the Reformation. It features five panels which depict the martyr being tortured with burning torches, poisoned by Athanasius and meeting the emperor Dacian at a heathen temple. The final two panels show his resurrection and the mounted saint victorious in battle over a fallen foe. At either end of the panels are statues of St George and St Michael, both standing over defeated dragons. The La Selle retable tells the tale of the saint in conjunction with that of the Virgin Mary, in thirteen panels, and avoids any reference to his torture. The work stands in a church in a small village and the absence of the saint's red cross suggests that the Norman patron who ordered it would have associated this symbol with the English army, and therefore had it omitted.

THE ART OF DRAGON SLAYING

UCCELLO

ONE OF THE earliest known paintings showing St George overcoming the mythical beast is Paolo Uccello's *St George and the Dragon* (*see page 130*). The knight is seen on a rearing white horse, lancing the creature, while the princess, in a corruption of the story, already holds him captive with her girdle. The fact that she already has him on a leash can be seen as evidence that the painting has a deeper religious meaning. 'If we reinterpret this image in the light of the identification of St George as a figure of Christ,' writes Samantha Riches, 'the princess can be read as a figure of the Virgin Mary or perhaps the Church, and the dragon is a clear representation of the Devil.' Through purity the Virgin Mary, or the Church, has trapped the Devil, allowing Christ to 'administer divine retribution for all his misdeeds'. The surrounding area is partially covered with rectangular patches of grass, illustrating the artist's obsession with linear shapes and decorative patterns, and the lance is drawn at an angle to create a three dimensional effect. The painting, c.1455, hangs in the National Gallery in London.

A much earlier painting by Uccello, from around 1439, shows a similar tableau but with the dragon (again with only two legs) standing taller and looking more fierce, while the princess prays behind him, taking no active part in his demise.

RAPHAEL

Italian Renaissance master Raffaello Sanzio da Urbino, better known as Raphael, painted two pictures of the dragon legend, as well as a connected painting of St Michael, during his Florentine period (1504–8). The first, now housed in the Louvre, is a small oil on canvas showing a black-armoured knight slaying the beast with a sword while a broken lance lies on the ground. The princess, some way in the background, flees for her life. The second shows the saint lancing a smaller, much less frightening dragon beside a praying princess. This later version was acquired by Catherine the Great and hung for 150 years in the St Petersburg Hermitage museum. In 1931 the Bolsheviks sold off some pieces and Raphael's masterpiece was bought by US banker Andrew Mellon, who donated it to the National Gallery of Washington.

TINTORETTO

The National Gallery in London's Trafalgar Square also houses Tintoretto's 1555 piece *St George and the Dragon*. The scene is painted from an unusual aspect as the princess, fleeing towards the viewer, is dominant. In the background St George is fighting the dragon at the edge of a sea or lake near a barely clad male corpse about to become the beast's dinner. Above the battle, the figure of God appears in the sky to encourage or congratulate the hero of the hour.

The painting is on a small canvas, suggesting it was for a home, possibly for a domestic chapel, and was first recorded in 1648 in the Palazzo Correr in Venice.

RUBENS

Flemish master Peter Paul Rubens was famous for his historical, mythological and biblical images and was heavily influenced by Italian art. While studying in Italy he examined the works of Titan, Tintoretto, Michelangelo and Raphael and was greatly affected by their style. While in Genoa in 1620, which has St George as its patron saint, he painted his version of *St George and the Dragon*, a stormy, dramatic piece with the knight, on rearing horse and arm raised, about to bring his sword down on the head of the dragon. George, unusually, is bearded, and the princess, again representing the Church, is shown in classical style, emulating much of the Italian work Rubens revered. The work hangs in the Museo del Prado in Madrid.

THE PRE-RAPHAELITES

The Pre-Raphaelite Brotherhood, formed in 1848 by Dante Gabriel Rossetti, William Holman Hunt and John Everett Millais, was a reaction against the mannerist, or unrealistic, style of painting made popular by Raphael and his successors. As a medieval hero in the truest chivalric terms, St George appealed to their traditionalist sensibilities as did the great knights of the Arthurian legend. Rossetti produced two beautiful depictions of *The Wedding of St George and the Princess*

Sabra, which took their inspiration from post-medieval retellings of the story of the saint, such as Richard Johnson's *The Most Famous History of the Seven Champions of Christendom*, which has the saint wed to the damsel in distress after rescuing her. The first, painted in 1857 and now in the Tate Britain, is a watercolour showing the happy couple in close embrace beside a wooden box which contains a dragon's head. The second, from 1864, was a design for William Morris, who was to copy it for a stained-glass window. It shows the saint and his auburn-haired bride surrounded by members of the court. The models for the scene were Rossetti's wife Elizabeth Siddal as the beautiful princess, William Morris as the trumpeter, and various members of the Rossetti family in the roles of the king, queen and St George. The stained-glass panel, executed in 1872 for Morris, Marshall Faulkner and Co., is housed in the Victoria and Albert Museum.

MODERN WARRIOR

On 23 April 2008 Canon James Cronin of St George's cathedral Southwark unveiled a new work of art by Scott Norwood Witts. *St George and Dead Soldier* expands on the theme of war by showing a muscular, balding and battle-weary St George kneeling in grief over the body of a modern soldier, who is draped in the saint's cross. Praising the work, inspired by Britain's involvement in the wars in Iraq and Afghanistan,

Canon Cronin said, 'We see the strength of character and we also glimpse the human fragility not always associated with the victorious St George.'

The artist revealed that his aim was to highlight the misery of war but he also wanted to alter the image of the saint. 'I wanted to change the identity of St George,' he said. 'He was a Roman soldier who put his neck on the line in opposing the persecution of Christians.' On another occasion Witts reiterated his desire to show St George as something other than a dragon-slaying legend.

> The painting *St George and Dead Soldier* has been inspired by British forces overseas and the historical misrepresentation of St George. As patron of soldiers and England, he is representative of both the military and the English people. This intimate portrait shows St George battle-weary and at odds with his traditional image, revealing the historical, factual man, a high-ranking establishment soldier whose Christian faith inspired him to put down his weapons and personally confront the Emperor Diocletian over his persecution of the Christian minority. Unlike the St George of popular myth, the historical St George sought peaceable negotiation to overcome oppressive forces and he put down his arms. This is the crux of *St George and Dead Soldier*.

The poignant painting was also displayed at St George's chapel Windsor during remembrance week.

ST GEORGE AND SATIRE

Throughout history cartoons and caricatures have been used to ridicule public figures or make political points. As the symbol of England, St George has come in for his fair share of this treatment, not least from the Irish. In the 1860s, as violence flared in Ireland, *Punch* cartoonist John Tenniel often drew the Irish people with simian features. *Punch*'s short-lived rival, aptly named *Judy*, pictured the Fenians as a dragon that St George had to slay. The satirical *Tomahawk* magazine turned that idea on its head with a cartoon entitled 'St Dragon and the George', in which a Fenian dragon impales the knight.

In more recent years St George has been used to represent establishment figures. One cartoon by Steve Bell, published in the *Guardian* in May 2000, saw the Conservative leader William Hague, in the guise of St George, riding a horse with the face of Ann Widdecombe MP, and spearing a woolly pink sheep. The caption reads, 'St William Taking on the Liberal Establishment'.

Epilogue

SAINT, MARTYR, hero, knight; whatever the truth behind the story of St George, he is a figure that the English can be proud of. For seventeen centuries his name has represented truth, bravery and justice, and he is venerated throughout the world. Churches bearing his name stand throughout Europe, the Middle East and Africa, and his feast day is celebrated in numerous countries, often with more vigour than the English can muster. He is a symbol which, far from engendering xenophobia, links the Christian and Muslim worlds, as those who worship at the interfaith shrine in Beit Hala will no doubt testify.

The romantic tale of his dragon slaying has inspired a multitude of literary works and endless retellings as well as countless priceless works of art.

In England, however, his fortunes have varied. While he was revered first as a Christian martyr, the Middle Ages saw the legend of his battle with the mythical dragon swamp the original tale. The Reformation further reduced his status in the eyes of the English and the twentieth century, with its religious decline and the rise of jingoistic groups adopting his name, damaged his reputation as a figurehead for the country.

Yet, even as England becomes more separated from the other countries of the UK by devolution, and Britain becomes further absorbed in Europe, pride in the nation and its patron saint has been steadily growing. Politicians, pop stars and sportsmen have joined the calls for greater recognition of the flag, the saint and the sense of national identity he represents. The push to celebrate St George's Day is gathering momentum and major upcoming sporting events, such as the 2012 Olympics, are guaranteed to produce an upsurge in patriotic pride.

Behind it all is one amazing multi-faceted saint who represents all that is good in humanity and the virtuous chivalry that the English once held so dear. With that in mind we should perhaps follow the lead of Shakespeare's Henry V and cry, 'God for Harry! England and St George!'

Afterword

The Rt Honorable David Blunkett MP is a passionate believer in St George's Day celebrations and believes the patron saint is a figure that the English should be proud of.

S T GEORGE is an important symbol because he leads English people to have an identity. To have an identity you need to be proud, and to be proud you need to refer back, not just to history, which is critically important, but to symbolic figures, whether it's St Andrew, St David or St George. These three each have a resonance in the countries that make up Britain – and, of course, the Irish have St Patrick, who is celebrated across the world.

One of the twists of this story is that the people who are most worried about celebrating our English identity are often enthusiastic about the Irish celebrating St Patrick's Day and recognising the sense of nationhood that the Irish have. I want the English to be able to celebrate both, to feel able to join in with other people's celebrations of their past, their present and their sense of belonging, as well as their own, but to do that you need to have your own sense of identity. I want to be able to feel a joint sense of belonging as both English men and women and British, and I think the two are entirely complementary.

Historically, the English haven't been as good as the other nations of the United Kingdom at celebrating their identity because for many years people saw Englishness and Britishness as synonymous. In terms of population the English are the dominant entity within the UK, as 50 of the 62 million live in England, so there has been a sense, as there was in the colonial era, that Englishness and Britishness were the same thing. But as the greater sense of identity developed in Scotland and Wales, and with the coming together of the Irish people, it has reinforced the need for us in England to feel that we too can celebrate English culture, English heritage and English music in exactly the same way as other parts of the UK are able to celebrate theirs. And I think that's a great thing.

In the past, the flag of St George may have been tainted by associations with the far right, but when I went to Portugal in 2004 as the British representative for the European championship, I felt we had captured it back, as we had at the jubilee. There were people of all persuasions not only waving the flag but signing the flag in the square at Lisbon, and that was a great symbol of nationhood. At the time of the jubilee we had people celebrating with both the St George's flag and the Union flag together. I think it's very important that we don't allow other people to capture the flag. We must be absolutely clear that this belongs to us as a country and we should be proud of it. We must put behind us the idea that it is jingoistic to feel proud of our own identity.

Does it matter that St George wasn't English? No, I don't think it does. It's one of those little quirks that he's possibly from what is now the Lebanon, or from Turkey. It doesn't matter. What matters is that he was adopted as a symbol and myths grew around him as they do with symbolic figures. The alternative to embracing that historic, symbolic figure is to have to invent a new one and I don't think we would want to do that.

When it comes to St George's Day, I'd like us to be able to celebrate it more rigorously. We wouldn't be able to celebrate it as a bank holiday, unless we were to do the same on 1 March with St David or on 30 November for St Andrew, so I wouldn't want to push it that far, but I would like us to do something as a nation and be much more forthright in celebrating. It would be great to see government, and by that I mean the three main political parties in England, agree on that and demonstrate that it is as special to us as the saints' days are in other parts of the UK.

When the next St George's Day arrives, I will be encouraging everyone to display the flag and I always encourage people, where they can, to have a party. I think we need to do more of that.

On St George's Day

I celebrate St George's day because it's my birthday but I think more people should celebrate it. It's good to be proud of your country.

TAIO CRUZ

BIRTHS

1564 William Shakespeare (English playwright)

1928 Shirley Temple Black (American child star and ambassador)

1932 Jim Fixx (American jogger/writer)

1936 Roy Orbison (American singer and songwriter)

1940 Lee Majors (American TV actor, *The Six Million Dollar Man*)

1942 Sandra Dee (American actress)

1947 Bernadette Devlin (Irish politician)

1949 Joyce DeWitt (American actress)

1955 Judy Davis (Australian actress)

1962   John Hannah (Scottish actor)

1970   Scott Bairstow (Canadian actor)

1983   Taio Cruz (English singer and songwriter)

1990   Dev Patel (Actor, star of *Slumdog Millionaire*)

DEATHS

1616   William Shakespeare

1616   Miguel de Cervantes Saavedra (Spanish writer, author of
       Don Quixote de la Mancha)

1695   Henry Vaughan (Welsh physician and poet)

1850   William Wordsworth (English poet)

1915   Rupert Brooke (English poet)

RUPERT BROOKE

Rupert Brooke was most famous for his moving poetry from World War I, in which he served with the Royal Navy Reserves. He died on 23 April 1915, at the age of twenty-seven, on a hospital ship in the Aegean Sea, after an infected mosquito bite led to sepsis. He was on his way to fight in Gallipoli. That he should pass away on St George's Day was somewhat appropriate, given his devotion to his country and the fact that his most famous poem, 'The Soldier', contains the lines:

If I should die, think only this of me:
That there's some corner of a foreign field
That is forever England.

He was buried in the olive groves of the Greek island of Skyros.

OTHER EVENTS

1348   The Order of the Garter was established by King Edward III.

1597   First performance of *The Merry Wives of Windsor*, by William Shakespeare, with Queen Elizabeth I in attendance.

1661   Charles II was crowned king of England, Scotland and Ireland at Westminster Abbey.

1815   The second Serbian uprising against the Ottoman empire began, shortly after the region had been annexed. The revolution lead to the establishment of a Serbian principality and eventually full independence.

1935   Turkey celebrated the first official Children's Day. It became a worldwide celebration in 1955 but had been moved to 1 June.

1979   3,000 anti-racism protestors convened in Southall, London to protest against a National Front meeting in

the town hall. Fighting broke out between the Anti-Nazi
League and the Metropolitan Police and the violence led
to the death of teacher Blair Peach, allegedly at the hands
of members of the Special Patrol Group.

1985 Coca-Cola launched the 'New Taste of Coke' after
changing its famous formula. Sales plummeted and
'Classic Coke' was back on the shelves within three
months.

1988 Pink Floyd's album *The Dark Side of the Moon* reached the
end of its record stay in the Billboard charts, after 741
weeks (over fourteen years).

1990 Namibia joined the Commonwealth as its fiftieth
member and also became the 160th member of the
United Nations.

1993 Eritreans voted for independence from Ethiopia (who
have St George as their patron saint).

1995 UNESCO'S first annual Day of the Book.

2009 Gamma ray burst GRB 090423 was observed by scientists
in the UK and US and lasted for ten seconds. The
stellar explosion occurred in the constellation of Leo
and, as its light took approximately 13 billion years to
reach earth, it is logged as the oldest known object in the
universe. The event was proof that stellar births and
deaths occurred when the universe was only 630 million
years old, one twentieth of its current age.

Timeline

270 Possible date of birth of St George

303 23 April probable date of death

679 First mention in Britain, by Abbot Adamnan in Iona

1000 Aelfric's *Passion of St George*

1063 Appeared to Normans in battle against Saracens at Cerami

1098 Ghostly apparition led an army against advancing Turks at Antioch

1099 Appeared at Jerusalem to aid Christians fighting Saracens

1191 Appeared to Richard the Lionheart at Acre

1260 *Golden Legend* published

1399 Feast day first decreed

1349 Edward III founded Order of the Garter

1415 Appeared at Agincourt and aided English victory

1483 First English translation of the *Golden Legend* published by William Caxton

1547 Guild processions banned by law

1552 Marking of St George's Day banned by the bishop of London

1589   *The Faerie Queene* by Edmund Spenser published

1596   Richard Johnson's *The Most Famous History of the Seven Champions of Christendom* published

1776   *The History of the Decline and Fall of the Roman Empire* by Edward Gibbon wrongly linked George to Aryan heretic

1908   Sir Robert Baden-Powell chose George as patron saint of scouting

1915   St George said to have appeared to First World War British troops

1940   George VI established the George Cross

1969   Roman Catholic Church downgraded St George's Day to an optional local festival

1996   St George's cross peaked in popularity due to Euro '96.

2000   St George's Day reinstated as a higher feast

Sources

BOOKS

Graham Bartram, *British Flags and Emblems*, Flag Institute, 2005

Sylvia P Beamon, *Exploring Royston Cave: A Simplified Guide*, Royston and District Local History Society, 1998

Paul Broadhurst, *The Green Man and the Dragon*, Mythos, 2006

Margaret H Bulley, *St George for Merrie England*, George Allen, 1908

Isobel Hill Elder, *George of Lydda, Soldier, Saint and Martyr*, Covenant Publishing Co., 1949

David Farmer, *The Oxford Dictionary of Saints*, Oxford University Press, 2004

Jennifer Fellowes (ed.) *The Seven Champions of Christendom (1596/7)*, Ashgate Publishing Ltd, 2003

Plantagenet Somerset Fry, *The Kings and Queens of England and Scotland*, Grove Press, 1990

C S Hulst, *St George of Cappadocia in Legend and History*, unknown pub., 1909

Richard Johnson, *The Most Famous History of the Seven Champions of Christendom*, 1596/7

John Mirk, *Mirk's Fesitval*, unknown pub., 1403

Giles Morgan, *St George*, Pocket Essentials, 2006

J Prawer, *A History of the Latin Kingdom of Jerusalem*, Bialik Institute, 1963

Samantha Riches, *St George: Hero, Martyr and Myth*, Sutton Publishing, 2000

Jacqueline Simpson, *British Dragons*, Batsford, 1980

Julie Spraggon, *Puritan Iconoclasm During the English Civil War*, Boydell Press, 2003

Gary R Varner, *The Mythic Forest, the Green Man and the Spirit of Nature: The Re-emergence of the Spirit of Nature from Ancient Times into Modern Society*, Algora Publishing, 2006

Jacobus de Voragine, *Golden Legend*, trans. William Caxton (1470), ed. F S Ellis, J M Dent and Sons, 1900

——— *Golden Legend: Readings on the Saints*, trans. William Granger Ryan, Princeton University Press, 1993, 1995

ARTICLES

Mall Hiiemäe, 'Some Possible Origins of St George's Day Customs and Beliefs', www.folklore.ee

Helen Gibson, 'St George the Ubiquitous', *Saudi Aramco World*, November/December 1971

Jacqueline Schaalje, 'Archaeology in Israel – Acco', *Jewish Magazine*, 2000

WEBSITES

www.berkshirehistory.com

www.eyewitnesstohistory.com

www.fordham.edu

www.heartkent.co.uk

www.heraldicsculptor.com

www.jacobus-de-voragine.com

www.kestrelsnest.org.uk

www.nationalarchives.gov.uk

www.nationalgallery.org.uk

www.ngl.nl

www.orthodoxengland.org.uk

www.parliament.uk

www.pinetreeweb.com

www.stgeorgesday.com

www.st-george-newbury.org

www.templarhistory.com

Acknowledgements

Thanks to Alan Rose of the Inn Sign Society and to the Royal Society of St George.

Special thanks to Ben Hamilton, Ben McKnight and Ann Sindall, and to Stuart Capel of CGE Strategy Ltd.

My gratitude also to the Rt Hon. David Blunkett for his time and input and to London mayor Boris Johnson for his contribution.

Index